TENNIS

TENNIS

Subhash K. Goyal

CRESCENT
PUBLISHING CORPORATION

[*The responsibility for the facts stated, conclusions reached and plagiarism, if any, in this book is entirely that of the Author. And the Publisher bears no responsibility for them, whatsoever.*]

Tennis

First Published : 2009

ISBN 978-81-8342-153-9

Published by :

CRESCENT PUBLISHING CORPORATION
4831/24, Prahlad Street,
Ansari Road, Darya Ganj,
New Delhi - 110002
Ph. : 23272541, 23257835
Fax : 91- 011- 23257835
e-mail : campusbooks@hotmail.com

Printed at :
Roshan Offset Printers
Delhi

Preface

Probably the most universal and popular of the racquet and ball sports, tennis is one of the great international pastimes. Played both competitively and informally by millions worldwide, the basic objective of the game lies in using the racquet to lit a ball over a net but within the boundaries of the opposite half of the court. Providing both exercise as well as sporting competence, tennis makes for one of the most interesting sports, being a highly organised field with widely followed and viewed matches, as well as tennis champions who are nothing less than clebrities.

This book in the series on sports has been designed as a comprehensive manual which gives the readers the basic information of the sport of tennis, as well as its celebrated players memorable moments. Beginning with a brief introduction to the history of the game, the book then engages in a detailed discussion of sporting paraphernalia of tennis, as well as its rules. It also gives the details of organised competition in sports, discussing the various championships and tournaments, the people who displayed their brilliance in the sport, and the defining moments which shaped tennis as it is today. In addition, it also provides a glimpse into contemporary tennis, equipping the readers with the most up-to-date information on tennis stars, games and tournaments.

We hope that the contents of the book appeal quite favourably to tennis enthusiasts.

Subhash K. Goyal

Contents

1

Introduction

Tennis is a game played between two players (singles) or between two teams of two players (doubles). Players use a stringed racquet to strike a hollow rubber ball covered with felt over a net into the opponent's court. Originating in Europe in the late 19th century, tennis spread first throughout the English-speaking world, particularly among the upper classes.

Tennis is now once again an Olympic sport and is played at all levels of society, by all ages, and in many countries around the world. Except for the adoption of the tie-breaker in the 1970s, its rules have remained remarkably unchanged since the 1890s. Along with its millions of players, millions of people follow tennis as a spectator sport, especially the four Grand Slam tournaments: Australian Open, French Open, Wimbledon, and the U.S. Open.

History

Tennis as the modern sport can be dated to two separate roots. Between 1859 and 1865, Major Harry Gem and his friend Augurio Perera developed a game that combined elements of rackets and Spanish ball game pelota. In 1874, along with two doctors from the Warneford Hospital, they founded the world's first tennis club to play pelota on the lawn behind the Manor House Hotel. The Courier of 23 July 1884 recorded one of the first tennis tournaments, held in the grounds of Shrubland Hall.

In December 1873, Major Walter Clopton Wingfield devised a similar game for the amusement of his guests at a garden party on his estate of Nantclwyd, in Llanelidan, Wales. He based the game on the older sport of indoor tennis or real tennis. According to most tennis historians, modern tennis terminology also derives from this period, as Wingfield borrowed both the name and much of the French vocabulary of royal tennis and applied them to his new game.

The first championships at Wimbledon, in London were played in 1877. On May 21, 1881, the United States National Lawn Tennis Association (now the United States Tennis Association) was formed to standardize the rules and organize competitions. The U.S. National Men's Singles Championship, now the U.S. Open, was first held in 1881 at Newport, Rhode Island. The U.S. National Women's Singles Championships were first held in 1887.

Tennis was also popular in France, where the French Open dates to 1891. Thus, Wimbledon, the U.S. Open, the Australian Open, and the French Open (dating to 1905) became and have remained the most prestigious events in tennis. Together these four events are called the *Grand Slam* (a term borrowed from bridge). The comprehensive International Lawn Tennis Federation rules promulgated in 1924 have remained remarkably stable in the ensuing eighty years, the one major change being the addition of the *tie-breaker* system designed by James Van Alen.

The Davis Cup, an annual competition between national teams, dates to 1900. In 1926, promoter C.C. Pyle established the first professional tennis tour with a group of American and French tennis players playing exhibition matches to paying audiences. The most notable of these early professionals were the American Vinnie Richards and the Frenchwoman Suzanne Lenglen. Once a player *turned pro* he or she could not compete in the major (amateur) tournaments.

In 1968, commercial pressures led to the abandonment of this distinction, inaugurating the open era, in which all players could compete in all tournaments, and top players were able to make their living from tennis. With the beginning of the open era, the establishment of an international professional tennis circuit, and revenues from the sale of television rights, tennis has spread all over the world and has lost its upper-class English-speaking image.

In 1954, James Van Alen founded the International Tennis Hall of Fame, a non-profit museum in Newport, Rhode Island. The building contains a large collection of tennis memorabilia as well as a hall of fame honoring prominent members and tennis players from all over the world. Each year, a grass-court tournament is hosted on its grounds, as well as an induction ceremony honoring new Hall of Fame members.

The Court

Tennis is played on a rectangular, flat surface, usually grass, clay, or a hardcourt of concrete and/or asphalt. The court is 78 feet (23.77 m) long, and its width is 27 feet (8.23 m) for singles matches and 10.97 m (36 feet?) for doubles matches. Additional clear space around the court is required in order for players to reach overrun balls. A net is stretched across the full width of the court, parallel with the baselines, dividing it into two equal ends. The net is 3 feet 6 inches (1.07 m) high at the posts and 3 feet (914 mm) high in the center.

Lines

The lines that delineate the width of the court are called the baseline (furthest back) and the service line (middle of the court). The short mark in the center of each baseline is referred to as either the hash mark or the center mark. The outermost lines that make up the length are both called the doubles sideline. These are the boundaries used when doubles is being played. The area between the doubles sideline and the lines next to them is called the doubles alley, which is considered playable in doubles play. These lines next to the doubles sideline are the singles sidelines, and used as boundaries in singles play.

The line that runs across the center of a player's side of the court is called the service line because the serve must be delivered into the area between the service line and the net on the receiving side. Despite its name, this is not where a player legally stands when making a serve. The line dividing the service line in two is called the center line or center service line. The boxes this center line creates are called the service boxes; depending on a player's position, he will have to hit the ball into one of these when serving. A ball is out only if none of it has hit the line upon its first bounce. All the lines are required to be 2 inches in width. The baseline can be up to 5 inches wide if so desired.

Types of Courts

There are three main types of court surfaces. Depending on the materials used, each surface provides a difference in the speed and bounce of the ball, which in turn can affect the level of play of individual players. The three most common surfaces are:

— *Clay* - red clay (used at the French Open), green clay (an example of which is Har-Tru and used mainly in the U.S.)

— *Hard* - examples are concrete, Rebound Ace (used at the Australian Open), coated asphalt (used at the U.S. Open)

— *Grass* - used at Wimbledon

Indoor courts are also used so play can continue year-round. Common indoor surfaces are hard, carpet, and clay. Some players are more successful on certain surfaces and are known as "specialists" for that particular court. Clay courts are considered "slow" because the loose surface causes the ball to lose speed rapidly and bounce higher. This makes it more difficult for a player to hit an unreturnable shot (a "winner") because the opponent has more time to reach and return the ball. Line calls are easily reviewable on this type of court because the ball generally leaves a visible mark. Courts are swept between sets, to erase any marks from the previous set.

Hardcourts are generally considered to be faster than clay courts. There are many different types of hardcourts, and, dependent on the construction of the court, can be relatively slow or fast. A fast hardcourt is characterised by low bounces, where fast-serving and hard-hitting players hold an advantage.

Grass is a fast surface and was the surface used at three of the Grand Slam tournaments until the Australian Open and the U.S. Open changed to hardcourts. Grass courts cause low ball bounces, which keep rallies short and gives hard-serving and hard-hitting players an advantage. This type of court also features unpredictable ball bounces, depending on the health of the grass and how recently it has been mown. For that reason, a volley from close to the net is a particularly appropriate shot on a grass court.

Professional players wear very different shoes for the three surfaces. Grass-court shoes are designed to grip the surface and prevent sliding. On a clay court, by contrast, sliding is an accepted and beneficial part of footwork skill.

Play of a Single Point

The players (or teams) start on opposite sides of the net. One player is designated the *server*, and the opposing player, or in doubles one of the opposing players, is the *receiver*. Service alternates between the two halves of the court.

For each point, the server starts behind his baseline, between the center mark and the sideline. The receiver may start anywhere on their side of the net. When the receiver is ready, the server will serve, although the receiver must play to the pace of the server.

In a legal service, the ball travels over the net (without touching it) and into the diagonally opposite service box. If the ball hits the net but lands in the service box, this is a *let service*, which is void, and the server gets to retake that serve. The player can serve any number of let services in a point and they are always treated as voids and not as faults.

Let services are extremely unusual, and placing more than one let service in a single point takes a considerable amount of skill or luck. If the first service is otherwise faulty in any way, wide, long or not over the net, the serving player has a second attempt at service. There is also a "foot fault" which occurs when a player's foot touches the baseline or an extension of the center mark before the ball is hit. If the second service is also faulty, this is a *double fault* and the receiver wins the point. However, if the serve is in then it is considered a legal service.

A legal service starts a *rally*, in which the players alternate hitting the ball across the net. A legal return consists of the player or team hitting the ball exactly once before it has bounced twice or hit any fixtures except the net provided that it still falls in the server's court. It then travels back over the net and bounces in the court on the opposite side. The first player or team to fail to make a legal return loses the point.

Scoring

A tennis match comprises a number of *sets*, typically five for men's matches and three for women's matches. A set consists of a number of *games*, and games, in turn, consist of *points*.

A game consists of a sequence of points played with the same player serving, and is won by the first player to have won at least four points and at least two points more than his opponent. The running score of each game is described in a manner particular to tennis: scores of zero to three points are described as *"love"* (or zero), *"fifteen," "thirty,"* and *"forty"* respectively.

When at least three points have been scored by each side and the players have the same number of points, the score is *"deuce."* When at least three points have been scored by each side and a player has one more point than his opponent, the score of the game is *"advantage"* for the player in the lead. During informal games, "advantage" can also be called "ad in" or "ad out", depending on whether the serving player or receiving player, respectively, is ahead.

A *game point* occurs in tennis whenever the player who is in the lead in the game needs only one more point to win the game. The terminology is extended to sets (set point), matches (match point), and even championships (championship point). For example, if the player who is serving has a score of 40-love, he has a triple game point (triple set point, etc.).

A *break point* occurs if the receiver, not the server, has a game point. It is of importance in professional tennis, since service breaks are rare enough to create a substantial advantage for the receiver in the men's game. The advantage to the server is much less in the women's game, but match analysts like to keep track of service breaks anyway. It may happen that the player who is in the lead in the game has more than one chance to score the winning point, even if his opponent should take the next point(s). For example, if the player who is serving has a score of 15-40, the receiver has a double break point. Should the player in the lead take any one of the next two points, he wins the game.

A set consists of a sequence of games played with service alternating between games, ending when the count of games won meets certain criteria. Typically, a player wins a set when he wins at least six games and at least two games more than his opponent. When each player has won six games a *tiebreaker* is played. A tiebreaker, played under a separate set of rules, allows one player to win one more game and thus the set, to give a final set score of 7-6. Only in the final sets of matches at the Australian Open, the French Open, Wimbledon, Davis Cup, and Fed Cup are tie-breaks not played.

Matches consist of an odd number of sets, the match winner being the player who wins more than half of the sets. The match ends as soon as this winning condition is met. Some matches may consist of five sets (the winner being the first to win three sets), while most matches are three sets (the winner being the first to win two sets).

Rules

— *No-ad:* The first player or doubles team to four points wins the game. One side does not have to win by two points. When the game score reaches deuce, the receiving player has the option to choose on which side of court they want to receive for the final game-deciding point.

— *Pro set:* Instead of playing multiple sets, players may play one "pro set". A pro set is first to 8 (or 10) games by a margin of two games, instead of first to 6. A 12-point tiebreaker is usually played when the score is 8-8 (or 10-10). These are often played with no-ad scoring.

— *Super tie-break:* This is sometimes played instead of a third set. This is played like a regular tie-break, but the winner must win ten points instead of seven. Super tie-breaks are used on the ATP and WTA tours for doubles.

Another, however informal, tennis format is called "Canadian doubles". This involves three players, with one person playing against a doubles team. The single player gets to utilize the alleys normally reserved only for a doubles team. Conversely, the doubles team does not use the alleys when executing a shot. The scoring is the same as a regular game. This format is not sanctioned by any official body and is only played when a fourth player is not available for normal doubles.

"Australian doubles," another informal and unsanctioned form of tennis, is played with similar rules to the "Canadian" style, only in this version, players rotate court position after each game. As such, each player plays doubles and singles over the course of a match, with the singles player always serving. Scoring styles vary, but one popular method is to assign a value of 2 points to each game, with the server taking both points if he or she holds serve, and the doubles team each taking one if they break.

Wheelchair tennis can be played by able-bodied players as well as people who require a wheelchair for mobility. An extra bounce is permitted. This rule makes it possible to have mixed wheelchair and able-bodied matches. It is possible for a doubles team to consist of a wheelchair player and an able-bodied player (referred to as "one-up, one-down"), or for a wheelchair player to play against an able-bodied player. In such cases, the extra bounce is permitted for the wheelchair users only.

Officials

In serious play, there is an officiating head judge or chair umpire (usually referred to as the umpire), who sits in a raised chair to one side of the court. The umpire has absolute authority to make factual determinations. The umpire may be assisted by line judges, who determine whether the ball has landed within the required part of the court and who also call foot faults. There also may be a net judge who determines whether the ball has touched the net during service. In some tournaments, certain line judges, usually those who would be calling the serve, are replaced by electronic sensors that beep when an out call would have been made. In some open-tournament matches, players are allowed to challenge a limited number of close calls by means of instant replay.

The U.S. Open, the Miami Masters, U.S. Open Series, and World Team Tennis started using a "challenge" system in 2006 and the Australian Open and Wimbledon introduced the system in 2007. This used the Hawk-Eye system and the rules were similar to those used in the NFL, where a player gets a limited number of instant-replay challenges per match/set. In clay-court matches, a call may be questioned by reference to the mark left by the ball's impact on the court surface.

The referee, who is usually located off the court, is the final authority about tennis rules. When called to the court by a player or team captain, the referee may overrule the umpire's decision if the tennis rules were violated (question of law) but may not change the umpire's decision on a question of fact. If, however, the referee is on the court during play, the referee may overrule the umpire's decision.

Ball boys may be employed to retrieve balls, pass them to the players, and hand players their towels. They have no adjudicative role. In rare events (e.g., if they are hurt or if they have caused a hindrance), the umpire may ask them for a statement of what actually happened. The umpire may consider their statements when making a decision.

In some leagues, especially junior leagues, players make their own calls, trusting each other to be honest. This is the case for many school and university level matches. However, the referee or referee's assistant can be called on court at a player's request, and the referee or assistant may change a player's call. In unofficiated matches, a ball is out only if the player entitled to make the call is sure that the ball is out.

Juniors

In tennis, a junior is any player under the age of 18 who is still legally protected by a parent or guardian. Players on the main adult tour who are under 18 must have documents signed by a parent or guardian. These players, however, are still eligible to play in junior tournaments.

The International Tennis Federation (ITF) conducts a junior tour that allows juniors to establish a world ranking and an Association of Tennis Professionals (ATP) or Women's Tennis Association (WTA) ranking. Most juniors who enter the international circuit do so by progressing through ITF, Satellite, Future, and Challenger tournaments before entering the main circuit. The latter three circuits also have adults competing in them. Some juniors, however, such as Australian Lleyton Hewitt and

Frenchman Gael Monfils, have catapulted directly from the junior tour to the ATP tour by dominating the junior scene or by taking advantage of opportunities given to them to participate in professional tournaments.

In 2004, the ITF implemented a new rankings scheme to encourage greater participation in doubles, by combining two rankings (singles and doubles) into one combined tally. Junior tournaments do not offer prize money except for the Grand Slams, which are the most prestigious junior events. Juniors may earn income from tennis by participating in the Future, Satellite, or Challenger tours. Tournaments are broken up into different tiers offering different amounts of ranking points, culminating with Grade A.

Leading juniors are also allowed to participate for their nation in the Junior Fed Cup and Davis Cup competitions as well. To succeed in tennis often means having to begin playing at a young age. To facilitate and nurture a junior's growth in tennis, almost all tennis playing nations have developed a junior development system. Juniors develop their play through a range of tournaments on all surfaces, accommodating all different standards of play. Talented juniors may also receive sponsorships from governing bodies or private institutions.

Match Play

A tennis match is intended to be continuous. Stamina is a relevant factor, so arbitrary delays are not permitted. In most cases, service is required to occur no more than 20 (ITF events) or 25 (ATP and WTA events) seconds after the end of the previous point. This is increased to 90 seconds when the players change ends (after every odd-numbered games), and a 120 second break is permitted between sets. Other than this, breaks are permitted only when forced by events beyond the players' control, such as rain, damaged footwear, damaged racquet, or the need to retrieve an errant ball. Should a player be determined to be stalling repeatedly, the chair umpire may initially give a warning followed by subsequent penalties of "point," "game," and default of the match for the player who is consistently taking longer than the allowed time limit.

In the event of a rain delay or other such proponent, the match must be resumed at a later time. On junior professional circuits the matches are to be resumed at the score which was at the time of the delay. However, as per new revisions beginning with the 2006 Australian Open, the ATP and WTA govern different regulations regarding delays; in the event of a rain delay, the match will resume while only the end of the previously completed set before the delay is official.

Balls wear out quickly in serious play and, therefore, in ATP and WTA tournaments, they are changed after every nine games with the first change occurring after only seven games, because the first set of balls is also used for the pre-match warm-up. However, in ITF serious tournaments like Fed Cup the balls are changed in a 9-11 style. Continuity of the balls' condition is considered part of the game, so if a re-warm-up is required after an extended break in play (usually due to rain), then the re-warm-up is done using a separate set of balls, and use of the match balls is resumed only when play resumes. It has recently been proposed to allow coaching on court during a match on a limited basis. Also, technological review of official calls made its debut in a major tournament at the 2006 U.S. Open.

Shots

A competent tennis player has eight basic shots in his or

her repertoire: the serve, forehand, backhand, volley, half-volley, overhead smash, drop shot, and lob.

Serve

A serve (or, more formally, a "service") in tennis is a shot to start a point. The serve is initiated by tossing the ball into the air and hitting it (usually near the apex of its trajectory) into the diagonally opposite service box without touching the net. The serve may be hit under- or overhand.

Experienced players strive to master the conventional overhand serve to maximize its power and placement. The server may employ different types of serve including Flat Serve, Topspin Serve, Slice Serve and Twist serve. A reverse type of spin serve is hit in a manner that spins the ball opposite the natural spin of the server, the spin direction depending upon right- or left-handedness.

Some servers are content to use the serve simply to initiate the point; advanced players often try to hit a winning shot with their serve. A winning serve that is not touched by the opponent is called an "ace"; if the receiver manages to touch it but fails to successfully return it, it is called a "service winner".

Grips

Players may use the continental, semi-western, western, extreme western or eastern grips during play. Different grips generally are used for different types of spin and shots.

Forehand

For a right-handed player, the forehand is a stroke that begins on the right side of his body, continues across his body as contact is made with the ball, and ends on the left side of his body. There are various grips for executing the forehand and their popularity has fluctuated over the years. The most important ones are the *continental,* the *eastern,* "semi-western" and the *western.* For a number of years the small, apparently frail 1920s player Bill Johnston was considered by many to have had the best forehand of all time, a stroke that he hit shoulder-high using a *western* grip.

Few top players used the *western* grip after the 1920s, but in the latter part of the 20th century, as shot-making techniques and equipment changed radically, the *western* forehand made a strong comeback and is now used by many modern players. No matter which grip is used, most forehands are generally executed with one hand holding the racquet, but there have been fine players with two-handed forehands. In the 1940s and 50s the Ecuadorian/American player Pancho Segura used a two-handed forehand to devastating effect against larger, more powerful players, and many females and young players use the two-handed grips

Backhand

For right-handed players, the backhand is a stroke that begins on the left side of their body, continues across their body as contact is made with the ball, and ends on the right side of their body. It can be executed with either one hand or with both and is generally considered more difficult to master than the forehand. For most of the 20th century it was performed with one hand, using either an *eastern* or a *continental* grip. The first notable players to use two hands were the 1930s Australians Vivian McGrath and John Bromwich, but they were lonely exceptions. The two-handed grip gained popularity in the 1970s as Björn Borg, Chris Evert, Jimmy Connors, and later Mats Wilander used it to great effect, and it is now used by a large number of the world's best players, including Andre Agassi and Venus Williams.

Andy Roddick uses the "extreme western" grip to create massive amounts of top spin. It is difficult to do this and could possibly cause injuries if done incorrectly. Two hands give the player more power, while one hand can generate a slice shot, applying backspin on the ball to produce a low and trajectory bounce. The player long considered to have had the best backhand of all time, Don Budge, had a very powerful one-handed stroke in the 1930s and 1940s that imparted topspin onto the ball. Ken Rosewall, another player noted for his one-handed backhand, used a deadly accurate slice backhand with underspin through the 1950s and 1960s. A small number of players, notably Monica Seles, use two hands on both the backhand and forehand sides.

Other Shots

A *volley* is made in the air before the ball bounces, generally near the net, and is usually made with a stiff-wristed punching motion to hit the ball into an open area of the opponent's court. The *half volley* is made by hitting the ball on the rise just after it has bounced, once again generally in the vicinity of the net. The *swinging volley* is hit out of the air as the player approaches the net. It is an offensive shot used to take preparation time away from the opponent.

From a poor defensive position on the baseline, the *lob* can be used as either an offensive or defensive weapon, hitting the ball high and deep into the opponent's court to either enable the lobber to get into better defensive position or to win the point outright by hitting it over the opponent's head. If the lob is not hit deeply enough into the other court, however, the opponent may then hit an *overhead smash,* a hard, serve-like shot, to try to end the point. Finally, if an opponent is deep in his court, a player may suddenly employ an unexpected *drop shot,* softly tapping the ball just over the net so that the opponent is unable to run in fast enough to retrieve it. No matter what shot it is, a forehand, backhand, serve or volley, putting spin on the ball, knowing how to use spin to its' best advantage, is what separates the top players from the rest.

Tournaments

Tournaments are often organized by gender and number of players. Common tournament configurations include men's singles, women's singles, doubles (where two players of the same gender play on each side), and mixed doubles (with a member of each gender per side). Tournaments may be arranged for specific age groups, with upper age limits for youth and lower age limits for senior players. There are also tournaments for players with disabilities. In the four Grand Slam tournaments, the singles draws are limited to 128 people for each gender.

Players may also be matched by their skill level. According to how well a person does in sanctioned play, a player is given a rating that is adjusted periodically to maintain competitive matches. For example, the United States Tennis Association administers the National Tennis Rating Program, which is divided into the following ratings (with higher numbers indicating more skill): 1.0, 1.5, 2.0, 2.5, 3.0, 3.5, 4.0, 4.5, 5.0, 5.5, 6.0, 6.5, and 7.0. Average club players under this system would rate 3.0-4.5 while world class players would be 7.0 on this scale.

2

History of Tennis

With the evolution of the racket, the tennis balls also underwent frequent alterations. The first tennis ball was wooden. It gave way to a bouncier, leather ball filled with cellulose material. The monasteries across Europe cherished the game during the 14th century much to the chagrin of the Church.

The game soon became very popular, predominantly in France where it was adopted by the royal family. During the period between the 16th and 18th centuries, the game called ' Jeu de paumme' - the game of the palm was a highly regarded by kings and noblemen. The French players would begin the game by shouting the word "tenez!" which meant "Play!" The game soon came to be called royal or "real tennis."

In 1874, Major Walter Wingfield acquired the patent rights for the equipments and rules for the game which bore close resemblance to the modern tennis. On the same year, the first tennis courts emerged in the United States. The game soon spread to different parts of the world like Russia, Canada, China and India. The smooth croquet courts served as ready tennis courts during those times. The original court devised by Wingfield was in the shape of an hourglass which tapered at the net. It was shorter than the modern court which we have today. His version of tennis courts and the rules of games underwent a fair amount of changes and amendments till the game gave to the modernized version which is played today.

History of US Open Tennis

The US Open tennis tournament, also known as "Open" or "US Open" is the fourth and the last event of the Grand Slam tennis tournaments. The tennis matches are placed for a period of two weeks, generally in the months of August or September, annually. The history of the open tennis is borne from two distinct tournaments-one for women and the other for men. The event was first held in August 1881 at Newport Casino in Newport Rhode Island. It was a men's singles tournament and it was called the US National Singles Championship for men.

The year 1900 saw the US Nation Men's Double Championship being played for the first time. The first official US Women's National Singles Championship was played at the Philadelphia Cricket Club in the year 1887. Ellen Hansel was the winner of the tournament. This was soon followed by the US Women's National Doubles Championship in the year 1889.

It has been a good 121 years since the first US open tennis game was played. It is the richest tennis tournament in the world with about $15 million as prize money and the triumph is definitely worth the sweat. The thought of creating the US open came to light after the US Lawn Tennis Association, founded in May 1881, volunteered to hold a national championship.

Twenty six players graced the introductory contest held in Newport Island, Rhode Island. It was called the US National Singles Championship. The members from the US National Lawn Tennis Association were only eligible to play the competition. The first singles winner was Richard Sears. He not only won the tournament for the first year but he was the reigning champion for the next six years.

The men's Doubles happened because the championship began to move around the country with nine different places hosting the event at least once. The men's doubles was split into an East and West competition. Clarence Clark and W.F. Taylor took the first doubles title for the match held in the year 1900.

The commencement of "Open era" (whereby players could play in all tournaments), in 1968, led to creation of the modern event as we know presently. Five different competitions were merged into one US Open Championship, held at the West Side Tennis Club in Forest Hills, Queens, New York. The prize money was at $100,000, and was shared fittingly between the 96 men and 63 women who graced the event. In 1970, the US Open was the first tennis tournament to introduce the tie-breaker system. By the year 1978, the tournament was shifted to its current home or the courts for the USTA National Tennis Center in Flushing Meadow, New York.

Tennis Scoring History

There are two theories which revolve around the Tennis scoring history. The first one states that the scoring has its origins in ancient numerology. In medieval times, the number 60 was considered auspicious or "complete" in a similar manner to which the number 100 is considered to be a "complete" figure now. The medieval adaptation of tennis thus considered 60 to be the "game" with steps of four points like 15, 30, 45 (or 40 as it is today) and finally 60.

The second theory is attributed to the presence of a clock at the end of the tennis court. A quarter move of the clock hand was made after each break with the score being referred to as 15, 30, 45 and finally 60.

History of the Tennis Court

The early tennis courts were quite different from the current day lawn tennis courts most of us are familiar with. The early version of the game is now called "real tennis" and England's Hampton court built in 1625 is still used presently. Courts of the present times are hardly used today. The court then was a narrow indoor court where the ball was played off walls. The net was five feet high on the ends and three feet high in the middle.

The year 1877 saw the All England Club coming up with the first Wimbledon tournament and the tournament committee played with a rectangular court and played with a set of rules that are associated with the modernized version the game.

Tennis particularly, the US Open is a test of skill, accuracy and agility. There is a huge amount of prize money to be won and a name to be earned for oneself. The game is popular with billions of people around the world. If you want to be fit and agile, grab the racquet and head out for an invigorating game of tennis!

3

How to Play Tennis

Anyone who is considering tennis training will be happy to know that there are plenty of ways to learn how to play the game. Every way from the tennis court to the internet, the video store and even the classroom will prove to be beneficial for those wanting to learn how to play the great game of tennis. Prices will vary depending on the type of training method that is chosen, but can often be quite affordable. This is especially true of those who opt for learning at home through the use of videos or internet lessons. A professional tennis trainer, however, will likely be the most expensive way to learn but will provide a hands-on experience that none of the aforementioned options can.

If you choose to hire a tennis instructor, you will probably want to hire someone who has a lot of experience in either teaching or playing tennis. Or, if possible, find someone who has done both. During this training, you will begin to learn the various swings and in which situation each can be used. In the beginning, tennis may seem intimidating because of the physical activity that is involved, along with the need to have a very fast reaction to every situation. But, after a few lessons, you will be more familiar with the game and how to play it. Patience is the key to learning anything new and tennis is no different.

Even prior to hiring an instructor, some new tennis players may decide to learn some basics of the game before beginning the actual lessons. This can be accomplished by either purchasing books, videos or doing some research online. Either of these methods should provide an introduction to the game, the proper way to grip and swing the tennis racket, etc. With this information, any new tennis player will enter their learning phase with added confidence and will impress their instructor by how much they already know. Not to mention, anything that you can learn beforehand may end up saving you some money on the actual lessons.

With that being said, it's important to know that there is nothing wrong with taking tennis lessons if you are a true beginner. Even if you have never held a tennis racket or held a tennis ball before, there is nothing to fear. Tennis instructors are there to help you to learn from scratch if that's what you need. During your lessons, it will always be a good idea to have access to a tennis court and possibly even practice a little in between lessons.

Many tennis instructors work one-on-one with their students, while others prefer to educate to a group of individuals. Those who prefer to learn as much as possible, but without doing so with hands-on training may opt for online lessons. The only drawback is that this method does not provide actual practice, which can be sought separately by the learner. Friends and family can often provide valuable insight in helping one to learning how to play tennis without professional instruction.

Basic Rules of Tennis

Tennis is a great sport that requires mental preparation and physical agility. The rules are based on the provided courtesy of the International Tennis Federation.

The Court- Tennis should be played on a court that is built to certain specifications. The court should be 78 feet long. For a singles match, the court should be 27 feet in width, and for doubles matches, the court's width should be 36 feet. The net should be composed of a net with a cord of metal cable supporting it at a height of 3 and a half feet. Service lines should be placed 21 feet from each side of the net, designating the area in which serving should be performed.

The Racket- The rackets used in tennis should only have one pair of crisscrossing strings. Vibration dampening devices are allowed on the rackets, but they can only be placed outside of the strings. No devices that incorporate batteries to help your play are allowed.

The Scoring- Tennis is a unique game in that it has special names given to the various points awarded. When calling out the score, the person serving the ball should always say their score first. A score of zero is called out by saying 'Love', and from there, the points go to 15, 30, 40, and game. If both players get a score of 40, the game must become a tie-breaker, and a 40-40 score is announced by saying 'Deuce'. In a 'Deuce' situation, if a player gets a point, they are said to have 'Advantage'. If a player with an 'Advantage' gets another point, the game is over. If a player gets a point while the other has 'Advantage', the score is reset to 'Deuce'. When a game is won, another game is begun until someone gets the best of 7 games. One catch is that they must win by two. If, at the end of 7 games, a player is up 4 to 3, another match must be held as winning by two is necessary. If a player takes the best of 7 games, winning by 2, they are said to have won the match.

How and Where to Hit the Tennis Ball

How to hit it is described in tennis as 'technique'.

Technique is learnt so you will be better in a match. The first thing you will need in a match is to get the ball over the net and into the court. The following basic advice will help you get the ball over and in when you are hitting forehands and backhands - otherwise known as ground strokes.

1. Hold the racket in a way that is comfortable for you. On the forehand, a good way is to hold it with the palm behind the handle (imagine you were hitting the ball with your palm, then put the racket there). On the backhand, you can use two hands or one hand. If you use two hands, probably best to have your dominant hand at the bottom and your supporting hand just above it on the handle, though not overlapping.
2. Watch the flight of the ball. Move to where it will be after it has bounced and after it has stopped rising. Reading the flight path of the ball is vital to move to the right place. ...The right place involves the following...
3. Stance - for beginners on the forehand and backhand, sideways on is good enough.........tennis is a moving game so try to get your shoulders sideways to the ball, even if you can't get your feet sorted out!
4. Contact point - try to hit the ball ...
   a) comfortably at the side of your body,
   b) slightly in front of your body
   c) between waist and shoulder high
5. Swing the racket at the ball ....from low along to high...make sure the strings are pointing where you want the ball to go as you swing - it is a bat and ball game, so use the bat to direct the ball!

To serve, the following advice is the basic stuff:

— Stand sideways on to the net.

— Throw the ball into the air so that it hangs nicely in the area where you want to contact the ball (see below for where that is!). The throw-up is also called the 'placement' coz that's what it should really be.

— The action of hitting the ball should be very much like a throw.

— Try to contact the ball in the middle of your throwing action at full stretch, slightly in front of you, and above your hitting shoulder. This sounds easy! Trouble is you can't do it if you've just thrown.... or even placed (!) the ball backwards and three feet away!

— If you get to the net, volleys are without hitting the ball, and the action should be a simple blocking action. Because you are at the net, you can use the power.

Where to hit it

A 'tactic' is a plan to win the point. There are five basic tactics.

First is to keep the ball in play - by getting the ball over the net into court. If your opponent can't do this and you can...you will win. If they can though...

.... Try to make your opponent move in order to hit the ball. Try to get them off balance or at least hitting on the move and test their skill on the move.

Whilst doing this...you will be better placed to hit each ball if you maintain a good position on the court before and after each shot. Be like a goalie defending the gaps - do not get caught out of position to one side of the court or stuck half way between the baseline and the net.

Once you can do the above tactics successfully, try to play to the weakness of your opponent ...this might be their forehand, but is usually their backhand.

Equally, use your own strength/s as much as possible. If you can use your strengths against their weaknesses... would be a fiendish plan to bring off.

Tennis Rackets

The single most important piece of equipment a tennis player will purchase is a tennis racket. With the wide variety of tennis racket brands, models, types, and specifications on the market, selecting a tennis racket can be a daunting task. Prospective tennis racket buyers should consider several important criteria. These criteria are brand, racket weight, racket length, grip size, balance, and head size.

Many tennis racket manufacturers produce multiple racket models with varying specifications. Popular brand name tennis rackets include Avery, Babolat, Dunlop, Fischer, Gamma, Head, Prince, ProKennex, Volkl, Wilson, and Yonex. Each racket manufacturer has its own unique characteristics and nuances that pervade their entire tennis racket line. You can consult your local tennis professional or tennis racket expert for advice on the brand of racket that is most likely to fit your needs. Ultimately, however, testing out different brands of tennis rackets is the best way to find the right match.

Weight is another important consideration when selecting a tennis racket. Most tennis rackets weigh between 8.5 and 12.5 ounces. In general, lighter rackets are easier to swing and players that lack strength (e.g., older players, children) will be able to swing lighter rackets faster, generating more power. The overall effect of tennis racket weight is somewhat ambiguous, however, as heavier rackets, while more difficult to swing, are more stable and transfer more force to the ball upon impact. Thus, when choosing a weight, comfort is the most important consideration. Typically, players that are more skilled prefer the stability and control offered by heavier rackets.

While the length of tennis rackets is fairly standard, many manufacturers have begun to offer longer rackets in recent years. The standard tennis racket length is 27 inches. While the rules of tennis allow rackets to measure up to 32 inches, most tennis rackets measure from 27 to 28 inches. The benefits of increased tennis racket length are increased reach and increased power. Longer tennis rackets can provide more power because the arc the racket travels during the swing is longer (especially on the serve). Players that are more skilled generally prefer the maneuverability of standard length rackets.

Because the grip is the tennis player's link between the tennis racket and his or her body, grip comfort is of supreme importance. Tennis racket grips typically range from 4 inches to 4 7/8 inches in circumference. Most adult tennis players use grips between 4 1/4 inches and 4 5/8 inches. The easiest way to determine your grip size is to grip a tennis racket and place the index finger of your other hand in the space between your fingers and thumb/palm. If your index finger fits comfortably, the grip size is correct. If your index finger does not fit, the grip size is too small. If there is a large amount of space around your index finger, the grip size is too big. Selecting the proper grip size on your tennis racket is important not only for comfort and for performance, but also for injury prevention. Using a tennis racket with a grip that is too large or too small can lead to arm injuries.

Tennis rackets are also classified by the balance point or how the weight is distributed in relation to the head of the racket. The two balance classifications of tennis rackets are head heavy and head light. Head-heavy rackets provide more power because they place more of the tennis racket's weight behind the ball on impact. Head-light rackets, on the other hand, provide more control because they are easier to swing and maneuver and absorb more of the ball's energy on impact.

One final consideration when selecting a tennis racket is head size. Typically, tennis racket heads range in size from 85 to 135 square inches. In general, tennis rackets with larger heads provide more power while tennis rackets with smaller heads provide more control. Players that are more skilled generally prefer the control and maneuverability offered by midsize tennis rackets (85 to 95 square inches) and midplus tennis rackets (95 to 105 square inches). Older adults and those who lack strength and precise strokes may benefit from oversize tennis rackets (110+ square inches). Oversize tennis rackets can lead to sloppy strokes, and are therefore not recommended for junior players.

Tennis racket selection can be a daunting process. However, understanding the specifications—brand, racket weight, racket length, grip size, balance, and head size, will help simplify the tennis racket selection process.

How to Grip a Tennis Racket

Many tennis players will not take a good look at the importance of their grip on the tennis racket. The expert will recommend that you restring your racket several times each year, but do not explain to the players that having the right grip is going to mean a lot when it comes to playing your game well and having the best tennis score as possible.

When you are shopping for a tennis racket, it is so important to consider the stiffness and the head size of it. Once you have made the decision you should make sure that the racket is the correct grip size for you. The most available sizes start at 4″ and will be increased by an eight of an inch.

There are so many different ways to grip a tennis racket. Depending on the level that you are playing at, you may learn one or more of the ways to grip onto the racket. There is the western, eastern, and the continental way of gripping. One of the basis ways of holding the tennis racket is to act is if you are grapping someone's hand to shake. You will see that this is a comfortable grip on the racket, which will allow you to have a better game. It may be weird at first, but once you learn it, you will get used to the feeling.

If you are feeling the need to increase your grip size, you can apply and over grip to your regular way of holding the racket. This will save you on the wear of your grip and will also give you a better feel. The good thing about over grips is that are not expensive and you can try them till you find one that feels the best for you.

It really does not matter if you are a professional or a beginner, you should understand the different grips and the options that are out there for you so that you can have a better game. If you are not comfortable with the grip that you have on your tennis racket, you may not have as much fun on the courts. You need to make sure that you have all of the information so that you can have fun and be good at the game too.

You do not have to be a complete professional at holding the racket. All you have to do is be willing to give it a try and have fun with it. You will see that you can catch on to the game quicker if you are holding the tennis racket in the correct way. You are going to improve your game and have more fun at the same time when you have the proper form and grip.

Improve Your Tennis Game in 30 Minutes

One of the most important things in tennis is to keep the eye on the ball. Nine players out of ten lose sight of a ball shortly after it crosses the net. It is essential to watch it until it comes in contact with the racquet. Most players, when they should be watching the ball, are either looking at their opponent or at the spot on their opponent's court where they wish to place the ball. The player who takes his eye off the ball, if only for the fraction of a second, may in that short time miss the opportunity for hitting it clean, i. e., in the center of the racquet. This applies to every shot in tennis.

It is an excellent thing while playing to repeat to one's self over and over again:" Eye on the ball," "Eye on the ball."

Many a volley and smash go out of court because the racquet has turned in the hand. This happens because the ball has not met the center of the racquet. Even a tighter grip will not prevent this. This difficulty is obviated by keeping the eye on the ball. Watch your ball and you are bound to judge it right. By hurrying and losing sight of it you are bound to misjudge it. Keeping the eye on the ball does not mean merely to watch it casually, but to reckon its flight, also to judge the speed and depth of the stroke. By doing this the player can tell beforehand where the ball is going to drop in court.

Another thing of first importance in tennis is to put the ball over the net. A player feels disappointed and angry at a ball that goes out of court. He feels the same way when he puts it into the net, for this has sacrificed all the chance he might have had of winning the point.

Again you see many players take balls which if let alone would go out of court. In doubles suppose you call "out," but still your partner takes it. If he returns the ball he at least has his opponent guessing and trying for a return. Many times he will be in doubt if he should take it, not knowing if the ball is going to be good. All this is that much more strain on his nerves.

Notice a first class player while in a game. He is always putting the ball over the net and at least two feet above it. The fault of the average player Is, that he plays his ball too fine, putting too many into the net in consequence.

In singles, because the opponent is more often playing deep, you should play higher above the net than in doubles, where one or both op- ponents are likely to be near the net. In gen- eral never play a return very low, that is, near the net on its way over, except when the oppon- ent is close up. Playing a return deep and well above the net keeps the opponent from coming to the net.

After making a bad return try not to get angry over your shot. Rather try to perceive at once what your error was and to correct the fault. It may have been your position instead of your stroke. Many a player blames a bad return on the stroke when really it was the fault of his position. For instance some players keep putting the ball in the net. If they studied their shots they would see that the thing to do was to get more height on the ball. There are many little faults a player could correct by himself if only thought of at the moment he makes them. Here are a few to remember and correct:

— *First* — Don't hurry; you have more time than you think if your position is the center of the court.

— *Second* — Don't take your stroke so close to your body that you cannot make a clean swing.

— *Third* — Don't try to kill a ball when an easy one would do.

— *Fourth* — Don't let your opponent find you out of position as a result of watching your own return.

— *Fifth* — Don't take your eye off the ball, as it prevents you from making a clean stroke.

— *Sixth* — Don't fail to "finish out " on your stroke in order that you may get a " drop " on the ball as it passes over the net.

All these little faults and many more which players have could be prevented if discovered and corrected at the time they are committed. Many players complain that they have not the time while playing to correct faults. One has more time in tennis then he is apt to realize, and this excuse is not a sound one.

Tennis Court, Dimensions And Surfaces

Tennis courts are standard in dimension, but vary widely in surface material. Tennis rules dictate the length, width, and placement of the lines on a tennis court. Tennis courts have a variety of surfaces and can be either outdoors or indoors.

The rules of tennis dictate that tennis courts be 78 feet long from baseline to baseline. A net, 3 feet high in the middle, divides the court into two equal halves. Tennis courts are 36 feet wide from doubles sideline to doubles sideline, and 27 feet wide from singles sideline to singles sideline.

Unlike the dimensions of a tennis court, the tennis court surface can vary in character. The different surfaces have different characteristics that affect the style of play. Common surfaces for outdoor tennis courts include grass, red clay, green clay, and hard courts. In addition, indoor tennis courts often have hard surfaces or synthetic, carpet-like surfaces.

The very first tennis courts were made of grass. While the number of grass tennis courts has decreased in recent years, some remain, and the world's most prestigious tennis tournament, The Championships at Wimbledon, is still played on grass tennis courts.

Grass tennis courts are considered a fast surface because the ball moves quickly through the court when it bounces. Typically, the ball stays low and close to the ground. Because of the speed of the court and the unreliability of the bounce, historically players playing on grass tennis courts prefer to volley the ball out of the air whenever possible.

Red clay and green clay are the two types of clay, or slow, court surfaces. Red clay tennis courts are made of natural clay or crushed red brick. The French Open is played on red clay courts. Green clay, the more common type of clay court in the U.S., is made of Har-Tru, a mixture of crushed stone, rubber, and plastics. Clay courts are considered slow because the ball bounces more slowly off the court. Typically, players playing on clay tennis courts prefer to hit balls off the bounce from behind the baseline.

Hard courts, the most common court surface in the U.S., are another fast court surface. Hard courts are made of asphalt or concrete coated with a thin sealer and special paint. Some types of hard courts have more extensive, rubberized coatings. The ball bounces high off hard tennis court surfaces and moves through the court quickly. Because the ball has a reliable bounce and the ball moves quickly off the court, players can employ a variety of tactics. Generally, aggressive play is preferred.

Finally, tennis players also play indoors, especially during the winter, on indoor tennis courts. Indoor tennis court surfaces are made of concrete or a synthetic or plastic material that mimics grass. Indoor tennis courts are generally the fastest tennis court surface of all. At the professional level, hard serves, volleys, and powerful ground strokes dominate matches on indoor tennis courts.

Choosing Tennis Shoes

Good tennis shoes do several things apart from covering your feet, and tennis is a sport, that is very hard on shoes, and feet, so you need to find a shoe that will last, and one that is not too heavy, bearing in mind some factors.

Tennis shoes must be able to support your feet with all the stops and starts you have to make, and it must give you good support at the sides of your feet. Each surface has differing requirements, and all of us have different types of feet, all of which places different demands on your tennis shoes.

The first consideration is what type of feet you have, because that will determine how much cushioning you will need, and what and where you will need lateral support.

There are three basic foot types:

1. Supinated– here your wear is on the outside of the shoes
2. Pronated– here your wear is on the inside around the ball of the foot, and this type of foot suffers the most with injuries from overuse.
3. Ideal– here the wear is even.

Either get a fellow player to walk behind you to determine whether you are walking with your foot tilting inwards, or outwards, or not at all. Better still find yourself a well-qualified sports shoe person. You could also test yourself by wetting your feet and standing on a square of cardboard.

1. If there is a large are where the arch of your feet didn't touch you are Supinated
2. If the whole of your foot is marked, looking like a rectangle with slight curves then you are Overpronated

3. If your feet leaves an imprint that is a balance between the others then your foot is Ideal

Confirm this self-diagnosis with a third party watching you walk, and the wear test on your current shoes.

The Fit of the Tennis Shoe is vital, and points to pay particular attention to are as follows.

1. You need about half an inch of space between your longest toe and the end of the tennis shoe.
2. The foot should be a comfortable fit without any stretching
3. The heel should not slip, although some movement is wanted.

Just remember your feet are different sizes, so pick your size according to the larger foot, and use an insole to balance up your smaller foot. The most important thing in a tennis shoe is Lateral Support because much of your running on a court is side to side, and there are dangers of turning your ankle. Good lateral support is necessary if you are heavy and if you are pronated.

Your tennis shoes will need a degree of Cushioning and Shock Absorption. This is especially true if you are a baseliner, and you play most of your tennis on hard courts. Pronated feet jar most easily.

The two most common cushioning you read about are EVA, which is lightweight, but not very durable, or stable, and PU[polyurethane] which is denser, better stability, but it is a lot heavier.

Flexibility is important, and tennis shoes must bend easily at the ball of the foot, however too much flexibility makes for a shoe that won't be comfortable.

Tennis Skirts

If you are not that keen on wearing the ubiquitous mini

skirt that is being forecasted as a sure-fire fashion staple for Spring 2006, summon up your inner athlete and go with a short, pleated tennis-inspired skirt made of comfortable, wearable sweatshirt fabric instead. This fashion-forward key constituent of the preppy trend will make you look sporty chic when a casual look is in the cards.

The 'tennis whites' look, however, is passé. The flirty, pleated white skirt may be considered a classic in the strictest tennis circles but you could alternatively add a little punch to your sporty wardrobe by going in for some interesting fashion variations. Tennis skirts are now available in a variety of sporty colors, silhouettes and cuts, and look fabulous in soft and vibrant hues like peach, aqua, olive green and ruby red.

This is a very informal sporty style, so it is best to pair tennis-inspired skirts with preppy items like the classic polo shirt or a tennis tee. Fashion critics advise not to pair it with sneakers off the court. These little skirts look great when worn with strappy wedges, Speedo sandals or even round-toed pumps.

Although fashionistas and others in the know often declare that for pleated and multi-layered skirts, the shorter the better, it is advisable to keep the length at mid-thigh and team tennis skirts with a modest sports t-shirt if you intend to wear it for a serious game of tennis. Indian player Sania Mirza was recently in the eye of a storm due to her midriff-baring tennis attire.

Tennis Tips For Beginners

Without first learning the movement and developing the skills for your achievement, you should take lessons in the basics of tennis for beginners. No matter how talented you may be, practicing consistently is the only way to stay in shape, and build technique for tennis.

The following are two basic types of stroke for people just learning the game:

1. Groundstrokes:

a) The player (or student) learning tennis for beginners must realize that groundstrokes are very important to master. A groundstroke begins with a slight, short backswing.

b) A possibility for you would be to also use a shortened grip on the club.

c) Use the regular type of follow-through.

d) Lengthen the backswing at a slow pace.

e) Slide the grip toward the handle.

f) Remember, in basic tennis for beginners, you will drop feed first! Second, doing your short drop feed is fine, and lastly, following the short drop feed, you will feed from your racquet.

g) Of course, you must start out inside the service line—and you may move back at rising pace. Begin slowly and usually try to end with a run.

2. Overheads:

a) The racquet must begin at point of contact and, again slowly, a bigger swing can be presented.

   1. The student should be instructed to stand close to the net—and then, taking his or her time, begin to move backwards.
   2. Remember to begin your student with an incredibly soft-feed right to the racquet.
   3. You can show them a few higher feeds at first—but do not do too much at once.

4. Especially for young children, keep your lessons brief and productive as possible. A child's attention span will not last too long. And you do not want to fail as an instructor by losing your student's attention. Sessions with younger students should not exceed thirty minutes at a time. Often it is good to set up lessons several times per week.

If a student is having trouble with drills—pull back and remember to work with individual students at their own skill levels. Tennis for beginners is sometimes more of a challenge with some people than others.

By the same token, if your student seems to be "a natural" and is having no problems with his or her drills—challenge them further—begin more advanced drills.

4

Tennis Equipment

Tennis has always been something of a fashion show. It began in the 1930s when Frenchman Rene Lacoste promoted his own brand of sports shirts by sporting the Lacoste crocodile logo on court. Now, tennis fashion is now a multi-million pound industry.

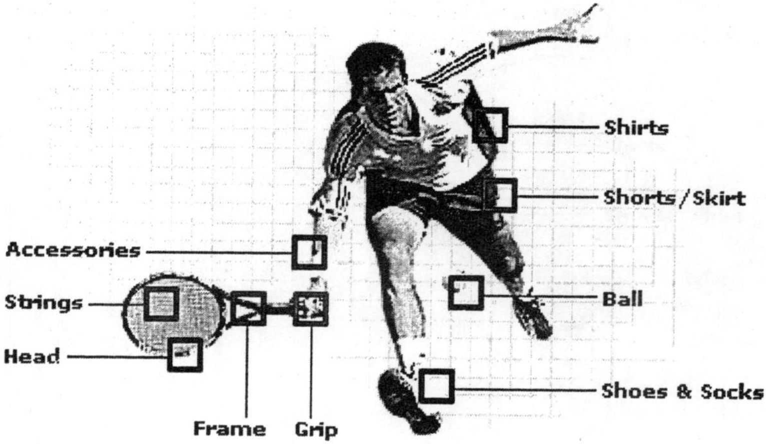

But specialist equipment does not have to be expensive. All you need is a racquet, balls and trainers. You could spend anything up to £800 on a full outfit and racquet. But you can pick up kit including a racquet for as little as £50.

But the racquet may be the one piece of equipment worth spending a little more money on.

Frame

— Racquets come in all shapes and sizes.

— The standard length for an adult racquet is 27 inches. A junior should use as long a racquet as she or he can comfortably handle.

— If it is too small, the player will have to use excessive wrist and elbow action - which is bad for technique and the arm.

— Once a junior weighs about six stone (38 kg), they are ready for an adult racquet.

Age 0-4 years: 19"
Age 4-6 years: 21"
Age 7-8 years: 23"
Age 9-10 years: 25"
Age 10-12 years: 26"
Age 12 years plus: 27"

— Go for a light racquet; which makes it is easy to handle.

— If it is too light, too much vibration will be transmitted to your arm.

— Between 10 and 11 ounces (280-300g) - about as light as a packet of biscuits - should be a good choice for a beginner.

Racquet Head

— Racquets were originally made of wood but most are now made of much stronger, lighter man-made materials such as aluminium or graphite.

— The only restrictions on the racquet are its size.

- It must be no longer than 29 inches (73.66cms) including the handle, or 12.5 inches (31.75cms) in width.
- The hitting surface must be a flat surface of criss-crossed strings.
- It should be no more than 15.5 inches long (39.37cms) or 11.5 inches wide (29.21cms).
- Most racquets are strung with synthetic materials such as nylon or even titanium.
- But the top players prefer to use 'gut' strings. Gut is made from the dried stomach lining of animals such as a cow or cat.
- Big racquets have bigger 'sweet spots' but are harder to control.
- A 'sweet spot' is the area in the middle of the strings which gives the cleanest hit. A mid-size racquet has a hitting area of about 85-95 inches.
- Beginners are sometimes encouraged to buy oversized racquets - up to 105 square inches of strings.
- Mid-size and mid-plus are usually preferred by intermediate and advanced players. A third option, mid-size plus (95-105 square inches), may be the best option as it will still be suitable as you improve.
- Most players should go for a reasonably slim frame to ensure reasonable flexibility (some pros like big thick frames which are very stiff).

Strings

- The best players use strings made from animal gut, which is the lining of the intestine.
- This is very expensive and factory-made racquets are fitted with a cheaper, man-made version.

— Professionals liken it to the difference between a Formula One racing car and a normal vehicle.

— Top players like Andy Roddick will also have all their racquets restrung after every match or practice session.

— Some will be strung very tight to give better control and spin, some much looser to give more power; so he can swap racquets depending on the way he is playing.

— The rest of us settle for the tension that was pre-set in the factory, probably between 58 to 68 pounds.

— One crude way to test if the strings on a new racquet are ok is to bang the strings on the butt of your hand to get a feel for their solidity.

The Grip

— If your grip is too big you might strain your hand, too small and you might damage your hand, wrist, or elbow.

— It is so important to find the right grip size. How do you do this?

— Hold out the hand in which you hold the racquet with the palm facing up and the fingers out straight.

— With a tape measure, measure the distance from the middle crease of your palm to the top of your ring finger (the one next to your little finger).

— This distance should be the same as the distance around the handle of the grip you choose.

— Juniors will measure less than four inches, the average women between 4 1/8" and 4 3/8", for men between 4 1/2" and 4 3/4".

— Like shoes, if you are a half size, you are better off going with the larger size, especially if you are going to grow into it.

— If the grip material wears smooth or begins to come away from the handle make sure you get it replaced as this can be dangerous.

The Ball

— Tennis balls are made up of a hollow rubber core and a wool or nylon shell known as the nap.

— In tournaments they must be white or yellow in colour.

— The rubber core is usually filled with pressurised air in order to make the ball bounce.

— The ball must be between 2.5 inches (6.25 cms) and 2.63 inches (6.57cms) in diameter and must weigh at least 56 grammes, but no more than 59.4 grammes.

— The rules of tennis say that the ball must bounce between 53 and 58 inches after being dropped on to concrete from a height of 100 inches.

— That is why balls are changed during tournaments - they begin to lose their bounce after about three hours of play.

At Wimbledon they are changed after the warm-up and the first seven games, and after that, every nine games. Studies have shown the fluffier a ball gets, the slower it flies, which is why you often see top players check several balls to find the least fluffy before serving.

When not in use, tennis balls should be stored in the can they came in. This won't prevent them from losing pressure, but can slow it down.

Shoes and Socks

— You can play tennis in any kind of trainer but if you want the best out of your feet, it is best to get shoes specially made for tennis.

— They have a few special features.

— Look for a shoe with a herring-bone style tread. This pattern wears slower and offers more traction than multi-purpose shoes.

— Reinforced toe-caps will make the shoe last longer especially if you drag your toe on the serve follow-through.

— Unlike running shoes, proper tennis shoes allow for side-to-side sliding. Added side-support is crucial to keep your foot stable even when playing shots on the run.

— Some players like to have extra ankle support, so mid-cut shoes are a good option. Breathable mesh insets in the leather will also make the shoes less sweaty.

— Women tend to have higher arches in their feet than men so female players should look for extra support underneath the arch.

— Choose cushioned socks that give extra protection to the bits of your feet that take all the impact - the ball and the heel.

— This spongy cushioning also absorbs sweat, taking it away from your skin making blisters and conditions such as athlete's foot less likely.

Shirts

— For a long time tennis gear was always white.

— There is logic behind this - white reflects the sun and is therefore cooler than dark colours, but in the 1980s, as competition among sportswear makers heated up, they began experimenting with all the colours, shades and patterns.

— Andre Agassi led the way with stone-washed jean-shorts and the crazy hues of his Nike-supplied shirts.

— This didn't always go down well - particularly at Wimbledon, which is the only tournament where players must still wear clothes that are 'almost entirely white' or risk disqualification.

— Now sleeveless shirts are worn by the likes of James Blake and Max Mirnyi, and the women continue to push the boundaries of tennis fashion, with more colourful, shorter and backless outfits.

— Serena and Venus Williams even design their own gear. But don't be swayed by labels when it comes to choosing your gear.

— For instance, tight-fitting tops may look good for some, but it may be more comfortable to wear a looser shirt which is more breathable.

SHORTS/SKIRTS

— Girls can choose to wear shorts or a skirt. But it hasn't always been so.

— In the 1920s female tennis star Suzanne Lenglen caused a stir - just for playing without a petticoat or corsets.

— Then Joan Lycett became the first woman to discard her stockings to play in bare legs and ankle socks.

— In 1932, Britain's Bunny Austin became the first top male player to wear shorts in tournaments.

— But it's all down to personal preference.

— If you are wondering how women hold a tennis ball without having a pocket to use, the answer is a ball clip.

— It attaches to the waist band and the ball can be clipped into it to hold it secure.

ACCESSORIES

— As well as a racquet, there are plenty of extra items you can be chucking in to your kit bag to help your game.

— Sweatbands to soak up perspiration are a good idea on a hot day. A cap or visor is also sensible, especially if the sun is low.

— But don't be fooled; many professionals are given headwear by their sponsors because wearing it guarantees their logo a place in the post-match interview.

— And don't forget the suncream.

— What about the essentials like the number of tennis racquets?

— Most professionals carry anything up to a dozen spare ones, each one strung with a different amount of tension.

— They will also carry their own home-made sports drink, often made specially for them by their personal nutritionist.

— A ready supply of bananas is a good idea - they make an ideal energy boost during a tough match.

— The rest of us can make do with a bottle of water, tin of balls and a tracksuit.

TENNIS EQUIPMENT TIPS

Using String-a-lings, also known as String Savers

String Savers are little plactic pieces that are inserted where the strings touch around the sweetspot of the racquet. They prevent your strings from rubbing against each other, and are intended to help prolong string life. String Savers are legal because the ball never actually touchs them.

String Savers are mostly used by players that have gut strings. They are usually effective at prolonging string life — but how much will vary. Some players complain that they fall out, particularly if they hit with a lot of spin. Some players also do not like String Savers because the give the racquet a stiffer feel.

Another alternative to lengthen string life is to use a thicker guage string. In any event, it is still recommended to replace your strings at least as many times in a year as you play on average in a week.

There is a little picture on the String Savers box showing how to install them, along with a tool for insertion. One box includes enough for one racquet.

What to do about Tennis Elbow

Here are some tips about what to do about tennis elbow. To alleviate a temporarily sore shoulder, elbow or wrist, a player can modify their racquet to absorb vibration. Try the following:

— String towards the lower end of the recommended tension range for your racquet. A looser string face will absorb more of the ball's impact. A looser face will also add depth to shots without a full-powered swing.

— Try a thicker string.

— Try adding lead tape to increase the racquet's overall mass. Adding weight will help reduce the amount of shock transmitted to the arm and hand.

— Check with your pro to see that your grip size is correct for your hand. It may be necessary to increase or decrease the handle size. Correct grip size can be an important factor in eliminating tennis elbow.

— Vibration dampeners generally have no effect on amount of vibration to your elbow. All they really do is make the racquet sound and feel different.

Nine Basic Facts about Strings

— Lower string tensions generate more power (providing string movement does not occur).

— Higher string tensions generate more ball control (for experienced players).

— A longer string length (or string plane area) produces more power.

— Decreased string density (fewer strings) generates more power.

— Thinner string generates more power.

— More elastic strings generate more power (generally, what will produce more power will also absorb more shock load at impact).

— Softer strings, or strings with a softer coating, tend to vibrate less.

— Thinner strings tend to produce more spin.

— Decreased string density (fewer strings) generates more spin.

Ten Basic Facts about Racquets

These facts are presented as generalities. While a stiffer frame generates more power, a stiff frame badly strung may generate less power than a more flexible frame properly strung for power players. While a heavier frame generates more power, it can also decrease maneuverability.

— A heavier frame generates more power.
— A heavier frame vibrates less.
— A heavier frame has a larger sweetspot.
— A stiffer frame generates more power.
— A stiffer frame has a larger sweetspot.
— A stiffer frame transmits more of the shock load to the arm than a more flexible frame.
— A stiffer frame provides a more uniform ball response across the entire string plane.
— A larger frame generates more power.
— A larger frame is more resistant to twisting.
— A larger frame has a larger sweetspot

Safe Racquet Storage

With the hottest month of the year now upon us (at least in the northern hemisphere), it is very important not to leave your tennis racquets in the car. Synthetic strings begin to lose tension at about 110 degrees F (43 degrees C). On a sunny, 90 degree F (32 degrees C) day, the temperature inside your car can soar to as much as 140 degrees F (60 degrees C) which is hot enough to even soften the resins in a frame and distort the racquet. If you are planning a game after work, take your racquet into the office; do not leave it in the car!

Racquet Stringing Frequency

One of the unexpected benefits of research in outer space is a design concept for a better performing tennis racquet. The essence of the concept is to taper the strings in such a way as to shift the center of percussion (also called the "sweet spot") toward the toe (the outer end of the racquet, farthest form the player's hand).

This concept originated more than 20 years ago in NASA studies of networks of strings for connecting platforms in outer space. Researchers found that changing the diameters of strings could radically change the stability of a network against vibration. This idea was inspired by an experiment in which a space-borne spider was coaxed to spin a good web and was observed to make its web with threads of nonuniform size.

The major difficulty in designing a high-performance tennis racquet arises from the difference between the position of the maximum speed (the toe) and the position of optimum vibration (the sweet spot). In a typical older design, the sweet spot is at the geometric center of the strung area of the racquet. The impact of the ball on the sweet spot causes minimal kick or jar to be transmitted to the player's hand. However, the average player tends to strike the ball farther out toward the toe, and to obtain maximum power on serves, it is necessary to strike the ball as close as possible to the toe. Thus, performance can be improved by moving the sweet spot outward.

In addition to increasing power on serves, tapering the strings to move the sweet spot outward improves the player's control and the feel of the racquet in the player's hand. An important element of improved control is increased stability: the racquet is less likely to twist in the player's hand on off-center shots. An important element of better feel is better absorption of vibrations; this is expecially important for players who have chronic arm problems.

The optimization of the tapers of the strings for a given racquet design is based on the fundamental physics of vibrating strings. A computer performs the optimization numerically, by use of a genetic algorithm. As its name suggests, a genetic algorithm implements a mathematical evolutionary process that resembles biological evolution in some respects and that arrives at an optimized design (disribution of mass along each string) by following a sequence of random design changes and preserving those changes that improve performance.

The string material can be nylon, animal gut, or other naturally or artificially spun threads. The sting can be attached to a conventional racquet frame. The required distribution of mass along each string can be achieved by spinning the string thicker or bonding different string materials along a central braid in the string.

5

Tennis Drills

Tennis drills are an important part of every coach's and every player's tennis development repertoire. They are used by professional tennis coaches at every tennis academy and every tennis camp around the world.

They are an invaluable supplementary asset in player development, from peewee tennis players to high level, advanced players. Drills can be used by two players or for large numbers of players (beginners or kids) in a group coaching situation.

Forehand Tennis Drill

One of the best forehand tennis drills to develop topspin is as follows:

— The player stands approximately halfway between the net and the service line.

— The coach stands on the other side of the net and throws (or gently hits) the tennis ball over the net towards the player's forehand side.

— The ball must bounce below net height.

— The player steps toward the ball using either a closed, semi-open or open stance to play a firmly hit forehand shot that must first clear the net, but then land inside the baseline.

By setting this forehand tennis drill up in such a way, the drill imposes on the player the necessity to hit a topspin backhand with correct technique as otherwise it's impossible for the ball to both clear the net and land inside the baseline.

The faster the swing speed the more difficult this drill becomes. Only highly advanced players are able to generate enormous topspin while still maintaining enough control to get the ball to land in. However, this drill is designed to enable the player to develop this ability.

This forehand drill is appropriate for intermediate to advanced players who have already developed the fundamentals of the forehand stroke.

Backhand Tennis Drill

One of the best backhand tennis drills to develop topspin is as follows:

— The player stands approximately halfway between the net and the service line.

— The coach stands on the other side of the net and throws (or gently hits) the tennis ball over the net towards the player's backhand side.

— The ball must bounce below net height.

— The player steps forward and across with his or her right foot to play a firmly hit backhand shot that must first clear the net, but then land inside the baseline.

By setting this drill up in such a way, it imposes on the player the necessity to hit a topspin backhand with correct technique as otherwise it's impossible for the ball to both clear the net and land inside the baseline.

The faster the swing speed the more difficult this drill becomes. Only highly advanced players are able to generate enormous topspin while still maintaining enough control to get the ball to land in. However, this drill is designed to enable the player to develop this ability.

This backhand drill is appropriate for intermediate to advanced players who have already developed the fundamentals of the backhand stroke.

Tennis Drill For Kids

A simple tennis drill, called "Two Touch" designed to develop the forehand and backhand volleys,, as well as touch and general racket and ball skills is as follows:

— The player stands in one of the service boxes between the net and the service line.

— The coach stands in the opposite service box on the other side of the net.

— The coach starts the rally by gently volleying the ball to the player.

— The player must bounce the ball off his or her strings, and then play back to the coach on the second contact.

— The coach repeats the process and both players keep the rally going as long as possible.

This tennis drill for kids is one that is both fun and effective in developing their ability to control the ball around the net. It teaches them to develop a "feel" for hitting touch shots, like drop volleys, drop shots and shots that require a certain amount of "feel"

To Develop Speed Around The Tennis Court

Utilizing a fundamental plyometric exercise, this simple tennis footwork drill for kids and adults is designed to develop speed around the court. The drill goes as follows:

— The player stands alongside a 6-8 inch plastic cone.
— Player then jumps sideways with both feet over the top of the cone.
— Immediately upon contact with the ground, the player jumps over the cone back to the starting position.
— The player continues to jump sideways over the cone for a total of 12 contacts with the ground.
— Perform 3-5 sets of 12 repetitions, with 1-2 minutes rest between sets.

Warm Up

Before starting this exercise, make sure that you are properly warmed up. Even though this is a very basic plyometric drill, there is still enough impact to cause stress to the ankle, knees and lower back.

Instructions

When performing the jumps, rebound immediately and explosively upon contact with the ground and back into the jump phase. The whole idea is for the feet to have as little contact with the ground as possible. When performing the drill, it's helpful to imagine that the ground is on fire and that you're wearing bare feet.

This exercise develops the thigh abductor muscles, stabilizers of the knees and ankles, and develops explosive power throughout the legs and hips.

Surface

Also, never perform this drill on a hard surface. Gym mats for indoor training and a smooth stretch of soft grass for outdoor training are recommended.

To Develop Explosive Lateral Movement

Utilizing a fundamental plyometric exercise, this simple tennis footwork drill for kids and adults is designed to develop explosive lateral movement.. The drill goes as follows:

— The player stands on the baseline where it meets either the singles or doubles sideline.

— Player then jumps forwards and sideways with one leg across the doubles alley.

— Immediately upon contact with the ground, the player jumps forwards and sideways back across the alley and repeats the process all the way to the net. From the starting point, try and reach the net with 12 contacts.

— Repeat the exercise three times with 1-2 minutes rest between each one.

— Before starting this exercise, make sure that you are properly warmed up. Even though this is a very basic plyometric exercise, it is demanding enough to cause an injury if the muscles are cold.

Instructions

When performing the jumps, rebound immediately and explosively upon contact with the ground and back into the jump phase. The whole idea is for the foot to have as little contact with the ground as possible. When performing the drill, it's helpful to imagine that the ground is on fire and that you're wearing bare feet. This exercise develops explosive lateral power throughout the legs and hips.

Agility Training

To increase your speed around the court, tennis agility exercises should be an integral part of every serious tennis player's overall training program. When combined with plyometrics, the result for you is a significant improvement in your on-court quickness.

A number of basic tennis agility exercises using an Agility Ladder.

— The player should stand at one end of the ladder, and then...
— Quickly place the foot closer to the side of the ladder into the first box
— The second foot then follows the first foot into the same box
— The first foot immediately steps sideways and forwards out of the box, adjacent to the ladder's second box.
— The sequence is repeated until the last box in the ladder is reached
— Perform 3-5 repetitions

Instructions

— Make sure that you are properly warmed up.
— Designed to improve your ability to change direction quickly, this exercise should be performed as quickly as possible. Ensure that contact is made with the front part of the foot, which should touch the ground for as little time as possible.

Progressive Tennis Drills

Progressive tennis is a special program that teaches young children between the ages of 4 and 9 to play the game quickly, efficiently and with success. In progressive tennis, the court size, balls and racquet's are scaled down to an appropriate size for young kids, and the proper execution of the fundamentals of the game is emphasized.

The following progressive tennis drills are a great way to turn your kids into lifelong tennis players while having a great deal of fun along the way.

When selecting progressive tennis drills, make sure to go for drills that aren't too complicated for young learners and contain variations for players that are more inherently skilled than others. Plus it will give kids a chance to track their progression throughout the season. Remember that these skills are not easy for some players, so always end each practice with a simple volley back and forth. Make sure to partner up kids with similar skill sets, and coaches can play with the lesser-skilled players.

Forehand for Kids

The first series of progressive tennis drills focuses on overhead strokes. To begin, have the kids stand in a line facing the coach with their racquet's raised to their shoulders. Teach kids the proper point of contact for the ball, and gradually introduce a bigger swing before proceeding to any actual hitting.

To start off, have your players stand approximately three feet from the net. Lob a ball towards the player and have them hit it using the point of contact demonstrated before the drill. As players gain accuracy, have them take one giant step back from the net and try again. Also, once players have the hang of the overhead stroke, try throwing a few higher feeds to teach them to extend their reach.

First forehand, now backhand

Once kids have gotten the hang of the forehand stroke, try teaching the backhand stroke with the following progressive tennis drills. First, demonstrate the motion of the racquet using a very short backswing. Some kids may find it easier to use a shortened grip at first. Once your players understand the motion involved for ground strokes, the drills can begin.

First, have kids stand three feet from the net again and one by one give them a drop feed to hit using their backhand stroke. Once they've mastered their returns, try giving a short toss feed, followed by a feed from your racquet. Another variation for progressing players is to start approaching the ball with a few steps, followed by a short run once the steps have become too easy.

Remember that these are very young kids you're dealing with, so they will require lots of patience and praise for a job well done. Any criticism given at this point must be done in a light manner. At this stage in the game, kids progress at varying levels, so make sure that each own player understands that they should only be concerned with beating their personal bests. Allow each child to set their own goals, such as ten volleys in a row or being able to hit the ball across the court, and write these goals out on large sheets of paper. Once goals are achieved, children will enjoy crossing their goals off the list.

TENNIS CONDITIONING DRILLS

When playing tennis, it is important to develop one's arm strength to be able to deliver smashing forehand and backhand serves and volleys. And how does one go about improving their arm strength? A series of tennis conditioning drills that will not only make your arms stronger, it will also help you game in the long run by developing your reflexes and footwork skills as well.

20 in a Row

The first of these tennis conditioning drills is for two players. Player one stands on the baseline in the center of the court while player two stands in the middle of the court between the net and baseline with a bucket containing at least 20 balls. Player two feeds the balls to player one with the aim of making player one run the baseline as much as possible. For each ball the player hits, they earn one point and for each ball they miss they lose one point.

Once player one has received 20 balls, the drill is completed and their final score is tallied. After practicing this drill for a number of weeks, players should notice their scores increasing as they gain arm strength and agility. When running this drill, coaches should make sure players are strictly adhering to the fundamentals of the sport, especially towards the end as the player tires from running.

Backhands and Down the Line Shots

The second of the *tennis conditioning drills* has players developing their backhands. This drill is for two players. To begin, player one stands in the center of the court on the baseline while player two stands across the court from player one. Right-handed players begin this drill in the add court whereas left-handed one start in the deuce court.

To begin, player one hits the ball cross-court to player two using a backhand serve. Player two returns the serve to player one also using a backhand. Play continues in this manner using only backhand to hit the ball. To up the competitive ante on this drill, the players can play a game where the first player to reach eleven points wins, with one point for each time their opponent misses the ball.

Finally we have a tennis conditioning drill that teaches players to hit down the line without landing in foul territory. This drill is also for two players, who begin the drill standing in the center of the court on the baseline on opposite sides of the net. Player one begins by hitting the ball down the line using their forehand. Player two hits the ball back to player one with their backhand, unless they are left-handed. If this is the case, they also use a forehand stroke.

The key to hitting the ball down the line is to hit the ball evenly and not too hard. This drill can also be played as a game in a similar manner to the backhand cross-court drill above. After one player reaches a score of eleven, players switch sides so that both have a chance to hit forehand and backhand.

Teaching Tennis Drills

The sport of tennis is gaining popularity amongst younger players, even those as young as 4 or 5 years old. When teaching tennis drills to kids, make sure to select drills that are simple yet focus on the underlying fundamentals of the game. If the fundamentals are taught properly at a young age, younger players have a much better chance of remembering their basic skills throughout their lives. The following tennis drills are a great way to put the fun back in the fundamentals of the game!

When teaching tennis drills to kids, always make sure to fully explain the drill first before attempting it, and allow players a chance to ask questions before beginning to avoid any mishaps or injury that may occur. Keep a close eye on your players and their balls as they practice, since errant balls can cause twisted ankles if stepped on.

Through the Hoop

First, we have a drill known as Through the Hoop, since it requires a hula-hoop or other large circle-shaped object. Have the players stand in a line with the coach standing approximately 10 feet away with the hula hoop in hand. The coach slowly lobs a ball to players one by one who attempt to hit the ball through the hoop. For every time they score a shot through the hoop, they earn one point. This drill teaches young players accuracy when hitting the ball. Players may use their forehand, backhand, or underhand motions to hit the ball.

When *teaching tennis drills* to your beginner players, look for drills that teach different skills such as the amount of power put into each hit. This drill, called Goldilocks and the Three Balls, has players introduced to the concept of soft hits, medium hits and hard hits.

First, demonstrate the "baby hit" by hitting the ball very softly, the "mama hit" by hitting the ball to the middle of the court, and the "papa hit" by hitting the ball full court.

Next, have players line up at center court on the baseline with the coach on the opposite side of the net. Lob the ball towards players one at a time and as the ball is in mid-air call out which type of hit you'd like the player to use: baby, mama, or papa. This fun drill has kids learning how to control the amount of power put into each hit.

Finally, we have a fun drill introduces the concept of the forehand hit by having kids hold the racquet like a softball bat. Once again, have your players line up on the baseline at center court with the coach on the other side of the net.

The coach lobs the ball towards the players one by one who swing their racket like a softball bat at the oncoming wall. To help children build up accuracy with these types of hits, assign a point value to a number of different spots on the opposite court, such as ten points for the back wall and fifteen points for a chair in each corner of the court. The player with the most points at the end of the game is the winner.

6

Biomechanic Movement in Tennis

When investigating the biomechanics of movement in tennis, one of the first things to do is to understand the movement patterns of the sport, specifically how these patterns relate to different court surfaces. Once these patterns are understood, we can design training programs that match the individual needs of our players. Famous German tennis coach Richard Schönborn, states that the whole movement potential of a tennis player is determined by the individual's conditioning and coordination abilities and that is why these abilities must be continually integrated into tennis technique.

Surface on Court Movement

Tennis is the only major sport that is played on a wide variety of surface types, including at the highest levels of the game. Fortunately, with an estimated three-quarters of a million tennis courts in more than 200 countries worldwide, few would dispute the inference that the liberalism that tennis has allowed in regulating the type of material tennis is played on, has contributed to the growth of tennis internationally and greatly increased access to the sport. Much of this work has contributed to the fact that tennis courts can now be classified according to their pace characteristics, which until recently was only possible through anecdotal reports from tennis players.

A recent study by O'Donoghue & Ingram investigated elite level tennis strategy and the effect both court surface and gender have. These authors timed rallies during the four Grand Slam championships, studying footage from 252 singles matches using a computerized notational analysis system.

Results of their study show rallies from women's singles matches (average 7.1 seconds per rally) to be significantly longer than rallies from men's singles matches (5.2 seconds per rally). Rallies measured at the French Open for both men and women were significantly longer than any other Grand Slam tournament, and rallies at Wimbledon were significantly shorter.

In addition to simply tabulating the amount of time of rallies for men and women during matches on different surfaces, these researchers measured the proportion of baseline rallies on each surface. This finding has significant ramifications on the dynamics and mechanics of court movement.

The proportion of baseline rallies for each tournament were as follows: French Open 51% of points, Australian Open 46% of points, US Open 35% of points, and Wimbledon 19% of points. These findings clearly illustrate the different demands and strategies employed by players on the 4 different surfaces used at Grand Slam tennis tournaments.

Findings by Grosser, Kraft and Sch nborn also show that in championship tennis, according to the court surface, a quarter to a third of all strokes are hit under time pressure (that is at least one stroke per point). Therefore, the influence of the various forms of speed on the result of matches is obvious.

Tennis Balls on Court Movement

New research studying the effects of the type III ball (larger) on court movement has recently been presented. Using a sample of recreational players, forehand groundstrokes were studied during rallies, with a particular emphasis on where in the court forehand groundstrokes were contacted. Results of the study showed that, with the type III ball, a greater number of forehands were struck in a position closer to the net, as compared to forehands contacted with the traditional size ball. Therefore, this research suggests that a greater amount of forward movement is required when playing with the type III ball in recreational players. Further research is needed to examine other characteristics and player responses when playing with the type III tennis ball.

Modern Technique on Court Movement

As young players developing, these authors were both taught to take the racquet back early during preparation for a groundstroke. In many cases, coaches told players to lead with the racquet as the body was rotated in a direction ultimately leaving it sideways to the net. In fact, Bill Tilden, in his book, *Match Play and the Spin of the Ball* stated that every player should:

- Await a stroke facing the net, with the body parallel to it.
- Play every stroke with right angles (sideways) to the net. This is true for service, drive, chop, volley, smash, half-volley and lob.

Again, recent evidence found by sport scientists and coaches during the analysis of high speed video has shown this traditional thinking of early racquet movement and side positioning to the net to be contrary to the modern controlled movement patterns of elite level players. Observations of elite players show that body rotation is actually initiated with shoulder rotation, most obvious by focusing on the movement of the dominant shoulder backward away from the direction of incoming ball, well before racquet movement takes place.

Early movement to a groundstroke is occurring in the lower body, with the initial stages of shoulder rotation occurring without substantial racquet movement. This initial rotation allows the player to begin trunk and shoulder rotation without having the racquet in an awkward or inhibitory position that would interfere with court movement. Players at early levels of skill acquisition will actually attempt to run or move to a shot with the arm and racquet straight out behind them in an attempt to prepare for a groundstroke. Careful analysis and observation of a player's initiation of rotation is another important cue for coaches and players.

Characteristics of Court Movement

It has been stated repeatedly in the tennis literature that tennis places demands on the ability of a player to move quickly in all directions, change directions often, stop and start, while maintaining balance and control to hit the ball effectively. The sprinting, stopping, starting and bending nature of tennis puts repetitive demands on the bones, ligaments and muscles to absorb the shear forces. Therefore, proper training exercises, including flexibility and strength training, are paramount for injury prevention purposes.

In addition, to enhance performance, players have to be in the correct position to provide a solid platform from which to hit the ball. This requires agility, speed and balance. Specifically, dynamic balance, or the ability to keep the center of gravity over the base of support while the body is moving, is important to the success of each stroke.

When moving the center of gravity to the edge of the base of support, you will start moving in that direction. When responding to an opposing player's shot, your center of gravity cannot be so far outside the base of support that you are unstable or over-committed. In tennis, the preparatory movement before such a quick change of direction is the "split step"

Mechanics of the Split Step

With continued changes in the game of tennis and the dominance of powerful exchanges from the baseline during points, players have even less time to prepare for groundstrokes during a rally. Early descriptions of the split step from the baseline, during the preparation to hit a groundstroke, reported both feet coming down from the air and landing on the court simultaneously. This maneuver enables the player to begin to move to either the forehand or backhand side to execute a shot.

More recent reports of baseline preparatory movement, however, have shown these initial descriptions of movement to be inaccurate. Elite level players have been shown to have a specific landing and foot position sequence during the split step employed from the baseline during a groundstroke rally. This information was discovered by sport scientists through analysis of high speed digital quality video of elite players during competition.

Using the example of a right handed player preparing to hit a forehand, the exact mechanism of this split step sequence will be discussed. While in the air and on the descent from the hop or upward movement at the initiation of the split step, players begin to time the landing from this upward movement by landing with the foot farthest away from the ball a split second ahead of the other foot.

In a right handed player preparing to hit a forehand, this would involve landing with the left foot first. As the right foot prepares to touch the court surface, elite players actually start rotating that foot toward the direction of intended movement toward the ball. This would specifically involve pointing the right foot outward in a right-handed player. This movement pattern is performed without apparent conscious thought, as players and coaches were generally unaware that this response or pattern occurred until recently. This exact mechanism or sequence is thought to enhance a player's ability to perform a lateral or sideways movement and may actually initiate rotation of the body toward the side of intended movement.

Examining the consequences or chain of events that a "toe-out" landing position on the side nearest ball has on overall execution of a groundstroke leads to a greater understanding of the importance of this sequence of events. Positioning and landing by the lower extremity in a position of external rotation (toe-out) serves to rotate outward the lower leg bones (tibia and fibula), which consequently rotates the upper leg (femur) outward as well. This outward rotation ultimately leads to a rotation or opening up of the pelvis toward the direction of movement.

This sequence of rotational events is common in nearly all human movement patterns and is termed the kinetic link principle. This sequential activation and predictable series of events confirms what sports scientists have described in sports biomechanics for many years. Clearly, much of these actions happen in a split second and can be difficult to detect with the naked eye. Therefore video analysis with stop action should be utilized by coaches and scientists to assist players in error correction and performance enhancement.

Mechanics of the Foot and Ankle During On-Court Movement

Additional information on movement mechanics for tennis comes from analysis and discussion of the specific mechanics of the foot and ankle. A common myth in tennis is that the game is played with the player on his toes or the balls of the feet. While tremendous loads are placed on the ball of the foot during walking, running and playing tennis on-court, examining any professional tennis player's feet often shows extensive callous formation on the toes and front of the feet. Slow motion video analysis clearly shows that tennis players move on the court using the same heel to toe progression as runners and other athletes.

Further analysis of how the foot and ankle move during tennis play also explains injury patterns and shoe wear patterns. Upon striking the ground, the foot is in a supinated position. Supination is a term used to describe the foot position where the foot and heel are turned inward, with a relatively high arch position. Upon landing, the foot immediately pronates or flattens (foot and ankle turn outward with arch flattening). This pronation is necessary for several reasons. First, pronation serves to absorb shock and provide shock attenuation to protect the body from the impact following heel strike. Secondly, pronation allows the foot to adapt to the court surface or slightly uneven positions, such as on a grass court or clay court.

After pronating while the foot is flat on the court surface, the foot and ankle re-supinate prior to pushing off of the ground. This is another important mechanical aspect, as failure to re-supinate prior to pushing off the court surface can lead to injury and non-efficient propulsion. Players who have very flat and pronated feet often acquire overuse injuries such as plantar fascitis, achilles tendonitis, and shin splints, due to non-optimal foot and ankle mechanics with repeated tennis play. Ensuring that players wear proper footwear and change it when needed, as well as applying orthotics (custom inserts) to the player's shoes are steps that can be taken to minimize the risk of injury during on-court movement and enhance performance.

7

Tennis Injuries

Tennis is a sport that places extremely high demands on the structural integrity of the body's joints. Athletes have to perform repetitive, asymmetrical and technically challenging movements at high speed in dynamic settings, often at the limits of their physical and mental endurance. It can become a daily battle against chronic injuries, which too often results in premature departure from the sport.

Among sports support professionals prevention and education at a young age are now seen as the key to decreasing injury rates. To entrench appropriate strategies within tennis organisations and educate players and parents is challenging, to say the least; yet it is not until we can do this effectively that we will see the results of our better understanding of injury patterns and causes. It is my opinion that if players are screened, educated and perform specific injury prevention exercises regularly from a young age, they will see a substantial decrease in injury over their careers.

A 1989 Danish study suggested that elite male tennis players suffered 2.3 injuries per player per 1,000 playing hours. Of these, 45% were upper limb injuries, 17% shoulder, 67% the result of overuse, 14% strains, 17% sprains, 2% fractures and 5% blisters.

By contrast, ATP sports medicine officials conducted a study of the injuries for which professional players seek treatment from officials. They found that 35-50% of all injuries were to the lower extremities, 20% to the upper limb, and 20% to the lower back. Players sought treatment for massage and stretching in 15-30% of cases. There are obvious limitations to this study: many players would not seek treatment from officials for chronic overuse conditions (which are more likely to occur in the upper body), whereas acute injuries are more likely to occur in the lower limbs.

A US study of 14 to 16 year olds in the US Nationals between 1996 and 1999 found some interesting gender differences. While the rate of injury was almost identical between girls (19 injuries per 100 athletes) and boys (18.4), the types of injuries differed markedly. Boys suffered more acute injuries, which was linked to their more aggressive and explosive style of play, eg much more serve and volley. Girls suffered more overuse injuries to the lower limbs, thought to be because of the increased time spent rallying from the baseline, placing more chronic stress on lower limb structures. The study called for further research on gender injury differences, as there is little data available.

It was also noted that most injuries, boys' and girls', were related to overuse; and that a significant number of those who got injured had sustained a serious injury in the previous year but had continued to train and compete. This confirms the need for better injury management and education, especially for young players. There has been a lot of media coverage recently reporting alarming increases in injury rates among the professional tennis circuit. Players have also been quite outspoken about the scheduling of their professional calendar and the lack of an off-season, claiming that they are struggling to meet the demands of the tour.

Lleyton Hewitt is a prime example of someone who has significantly cut back his schedule to focus on longevity in the game. Other reasons offered for increased injury incidence include the speed of the game and the power that can be delivered from modern racquets. However, a study conducted by the ATP sports medicine trainer Doug Spreen, does not exactly confirm this supposed injury trend. Spreen found only incremental increases in injury rates among players between 1995 and 2000, measured in terms of withdrawals from tournaments before the start and retirements from matches. In the players' defence, it would be reasonable to query how far this study would have reflected the incidence of chronic injuries, as they are less likely to have come to the attention of the ATP's trainers. Regardless, we need more elite level research, during both tournaments and training, to determine whether or not the overall injury rate (both chronic and acute) is in fact increasing, as suggested by the media and the players.

Acute Injuries

It is inevitable that in a sport where players are accelerating, stopping, turning and lunging for anything from one to five hours, acute injuries occur. Most acute lower-limb joint injuries are minor compared to what is seen in contact sports such as football. Acute ankle sprains, low grade knee ligament sprains and meniscal injuries to the knee are common. Although muscle strains are seen, they are also far less common than in sports such as Australian Rules Football or rugby, as players rarely run more then 10 steps in one direction and therefore never really use the full sprinting stride that puts the hamstring and rectus femoris muscles under high load. Nor are athletes required to kick, which we all know is a predisposing factor for muscle strains.

Calf muscle strains are common among older social athletes. Among adolescents, it is essential during assessments (as in any sport demanding dynamic and powerful movements) to consider the possibility of avulsion injuries at muscle insertion sites. The most common acute injury site in the upper limb is the wrist. A perfect example of how wrist injuries happen was Boris Becker at Wimbledon in 1996, stretching for a wide forehand return which he mistimed, forcing his wrist into hyperextension with rotation and leading to his subsequent withdrawal from the tournament. Although acute injuries are hard to predict and prevent, measures can still be taken to reduce the risk, such as proprioceptive and strength training for susceptible joints, advice on bracing and taping, and ensuring the player is using the right equipment.

Use of Equipment

The technology behind tennis and the equipment used is continually evolving and support professionals must be aware of the impact it can have on a presenting injury. It is always hard for non-players of a sport to appreciate how subtle variations in equipment can change the load on a player's body, so when searching for underlying causes, be sure to question the player about any recent changes in equipment.

Racquet type can be critical, particularly with juniors, who make frequent changes as they grow out of their racquets and are influenced by new trends. The stiffness of the racquet is paramount: if it is too stiff for the particular player, it can cause upper-limb injuries. Often juniors select racquets that are too stiff for their physical development. Professionals usually aim for a stiff racquet because it provides them with more feel; but juniors need flexibility in the racquet so that the shock on impact is dispersed.

String tension has the same effect. As players get older, their increased physical strength means they need less assistance from the racquet to produce power at contact and they generally increase their string tension in their quest for more control. Juniors should make these increases in small increments, but they often do it in big jumps, to the detriment of their wrists, elbows or shoulders.

You should also consider the type of string being used. In the past 10 years some very stiff string types have come into use, which are very popular for the power and durability they deliver. But they do increase shock through the upper limb on contact. Finally, in terms of racquet set-up, is the grip size. In tennis, you should play with a relaxed feel on the racquet. A grip too big or small will increase grip tension and the likelihood of elbow and wrist injuries, as well as impeding a fluent swing.

For anyone who presents with lateral epicondylitis (tennis elbow, see below), you must take an in-depth look at their racquet set-up. This is particularly important for middle-aged women, where the prevalence is high. The correct grip size, a flexible racquet and string type and quite loose string tension are essential for this group.

The ATP study also analysed the impact on injuries of the court surface, finding clay far more forgiving than grass or hard court, with 0.2 treatments per match on clay compared with 0.37 and 0.42 on hard court and grass respectively. Clay is a slower, softer surface, encouraging a less explosive style of tennis, and this was seen as the reason behind the lesser injury rate. Artificial grass, commonly seen at local tennis clubs, has similar qualities to clay.

Support professionals should take note of this in their advice, especially to older players, who are often in a position to be able to choose their training and playing surfaces, and who usually need a surface that helps to offload lower limb joints.

Prevention of Chronic injuries

The prevention of overuse injuries is where we as sports medicine practitioners can have a profound effect on the careers of promising young players. Succumbing to injury can blight a career in its early stages: because tennis depends on the cumulative effect of training specific neural patterns, prolonged periods of rest can interrupt this process to the long-term detriment of the athlete's technical competence. A 14 year old suffering from chronic shoulder tendinitis with underlying instability and changes in joint range of movement may have to limit his or her serving for three to six months while making the necessary changes to the joint in rehabilitation. This comes at a point when physical development is usually peaking and when the young athlete's serve will be undergoing critical changes.

Most coaches don't understand injury presentations and the progressive nature of overuse injuries with continual overload and subsequent loss of joint integrity. It is our job when managing the injury of a young player to ensure that coaches are aiming at quality, not quantity, in their training programmes, particularly with serving practice. The notion of a youngster serving basket after basket of balls, or a coach training a youngster on court until he or she drops, is no longer acceptable. The risk of injury is too great and in a sport as technical as tennis, heightened fatigue just leads to the training of incorrect neural pathways (ie, bad habits), which will further compromise joints.

The emphasis needs to be on replicating the correct technique during training for each stroke, and this is only possible by ensuring the athlete has a sufficient recovery period between training drills, especially for athletes with a particular injury concern. For older players, the chronic injury concerns are somewhat different. A prime example is tennis elbow or lateral epicondylitis – far more common among older players than the young, in my experience.

The typical presentation is an elderly female with a single-handed backhand who leads with the elbow and straightens the elbow and extends the wrist on contact, placing the wrist extensors under excessive tension (rather than swinging from the shoulder with a straight arm and using the entire body to execute the stroke). With tennis elbow, you will need to look at the cervical and thoracic spine, as there is usually some associated dysfunction in this area.

Not surprisingly, injuries to the lumbar spine, shoulder and knees are generally more down to degeneration and stiffness in older people. Among serious tennis players there are five key areas of susceptibility for overuse injuries: shoulder, medial elbow, wrist, lumbar spine and anterior knee complex. Injury prevention programmes for young athletes should target key areas of flexibility and strength at these joints and should, for any serious young player, be started by the age of 12.

Tennis Injury and Sprinting Injury Prevention Exercises

Tennis-related injuries are common at all levels of the game - junior, recreational or pro tour. One of the most frequent is the infamous 'tennis elbow'. This is a typical chronic overuse injury. It seems to be associated with lack of forearm strength, or more specifically a strength imbalance between the wrist extensor muscles and wrist flexor muscles. This is particularly true of junior players who suffer from this problem. It is also associated with poor technique, relying on too much arm power to make the shots rather than body rotation. This arm-dominant technique places too much stress on the elbow and wrist joints and hence the injury. This technique-related cause is most common in recreational players.

A second frequently seen chronic overuse injury in tennis is shoulder tendinitis. This is often a rotator-cuff impingement injury caused by repeated overhead and inward rotation movements of the arm. This leads to a dominance of the anterior deltoid and pectoralis muscles and a relative weakening of the rotator cuff in rear-shoulder girdle muscles. Mechanically this leads to an increasingly unstable and weak positioning of the shoulder joint, which stresses the tendons.

Watch your Back

Back injuries are also common in tennis. In élite players, who have played many hours a week for many years, it is common to see right versus left side strength imbalances. Players have a dominant arm which leads to a dominant trunk rotation movement. Players often have a dominant leg which they are more comfortable balancing or moving on, which leads to a dominant hip movement. These imbalances can cause low-back problems if the player does not have the required core stability. In addition, many tennis shots and movements involve back extension and flexion, placing a lot of stress on the back musculature. Without sufficient strength and flexibility in the hips and spine, an élite player may overload the back.

For recreational players, poor posture and insufficient core stability may lead to back problems when they play tennis. In this case, though, tennis would not be the primary cause of the injury but simply the activity that sets off symptoms. Other injuries in tennis are knee and ankle sprains. These are acute-accident injuries which are hard to avoid. However, an élite player would need to ensure sufficient strength in the leg muscles and develop good balance and movement skills to decrease the likelihood of a sprain. While sprains are accidents, common sense says that a strong, well balanced and agile player is at less risk than a weak, poorly coordinated player.

Injury prevention strategies

The most basic strategy for preventing tennis injuries, particularly back, shoulder and elbow problems, is to avoid overuse. This means not playing too much or too frequently, or not increasing the amount you play too quickly. Most recreational players will be able to play once or twice a week and avoid any shoulder or elbow problems, but if they increased this, then poor technique and lack of conditioning training would increase their injury risk dramatically. For the aspiring junior player or full-time pro, who have to play most days, the only way to prevent injuries is with a suitable conditioning programme. The following programme focuses on the elements a tennis player would need to avoid injury. These exercises are not meant to be definitive, but the muscles and movements that are being trained here are well designed to gain optimal benefits. Use this example to guide you in your own conditioning programme.

Flexibility training

Everyday stretches for the following muscle groups must be performed. The goal is to achieve a good range of motion in all major joints: calf; hamstrings; quadriceps; hip flexors; groin; gluteals; low back flexors; upper back extensors; trunk rotators; pectorals; shoulder rotators; rear shoulders; triceps and forearms.

General strength training

For players who do not have a strong background in conditioning training, a workout like the following should be completed 2-3 times a week to develop a well-balanced all-body strength. For players who are already strong, this type of workout can be used once a week to maintain general strength levels year-round, or 2-3 times a week in a general phase a few times each year.

Perform 3 sets x 8-12 reps of the following:

— dumbbell shoulder press

— single arm dumbbell row

— lat pull downs

— barbell squats

— lunges.

Build up to 3-4 sets of 20 reps of the following:

— crunches.

— back extensions.

Core-stability training

Players must be able to isolate the transversus abdominis muscle and perform the abdominal hollowing exercise correctly. They must also be able to maintain a 'neutral' lumbar spine position during various movements. Primarily this involves recruiting 'tranversus' effectively along with other trunk and hip stability muscles. Exercise examples are: while lying on back lift one leg; while standing lift one leg; while standing up lean forward from the hips; while kneeling on all fours extend the leg behind.

Players need to be able to use the gluteal muscles to stabilise the pelvis. Bridging exercises and hip extension movements focusing on gluteal recruitment over the back and hamstring muscles should be performed.

Once the above basic skills are mastered, dynamic exercises such as the one-leg squat, while keeping the lumbar spine in neutral and the pelvis stable, will develop the ability of the player to maintain stability during movement on court.

Also useful are cable rotation exercises using a pulley machine. The player mimics the forehand and backhand movement while maintaining good posture and core stability through the rotation movement. These exercise suggestions will ensure that the core-stability skills are transferred onto the court. It is always important to remember that sports-specific training is important to help athletes prevent injuries effectively.

Specific conditioning for shoulder and arm

The following exercises will help develop strong shoulder rotator cuff and forearm muscles to help prevent elbow and shoulder tendinitis injuries:

1. Side-lying raise. 3 x 15. Lie on side. Using top arm, lift dumbbell up to 45 degrees. Lower slowly.
2. Band /cable external rotations. 3 x 15. Stand and grasp band/cable in hand. With elbow tucked into your ribs rotate the arm out, pulling against the resistance.
3. Russian arm circles. 3 x 15. Lie on front. Start with arms straight out above head, lift them off the floor and pull them down to your sides. Keeping them off the floor at all times continue to make big circles with your arms up and down. Progress to using small weights.
4. Modified lat raise. 3 x15. Perform a lateral raise movement with palms facing back and thumbs down. Lift your elbows to about 60 degrees to your sides only.

5. Wrist extensions. 3 x 15. Sit and place your forearm on your thigh with your elbow bent. With your palm facing down, grasp a dumbbell in your hand. Lift the weight pulling the back of your hand up by using the upper forearm muscles.
6. Band wrist supinations and pronations. 3 x 15. Supination: Position as 5 but grasp a resistance band and secure the other end of the band under your foot. Grasp the band between your thumb and hand with palm down. Rotate your wrist so the palm faces up. Slowly rotate back and continue.

Pronation: Change grip so that you grasp the band between your thumb and hand with palm up and rotate your wrist so the palm faces down.

Sprinting injuries

As you might imagine, most sprinting injuries involve the legs, with hamstring and calf strains and Achilles tendinitis being among the most common. Lower-back problems are also frequent and knee injuries can occur as well. Knee injuries tend to be quadriceps tendinitis or patella tendinitis type injuries. The reason why most of the injuries are muscle strains or tendinitis type is that sprinting involves high forces and a large range of motion which place the muscles under great stress. Sprinting is a linear running sport and obviously involves no contact, so there are few knee or ankle joint sprain injuries.

An important example of the high muscle forces involved in sprinting is the function of the hamstrings. During the sprint running action the hamstrings have two roles to play. The first role is to contract eccentrically as a knee flexor just before footstrike and, in the first part of ground contact, to control the knee extension force of the quadriceps and stabilise the knee for the ground impact force. Second, during the second half of the stance phase the hamstring contracts concentrically, this time as a hip extensor, powerfully driving the leg backwards. This concentric hip extension force from the hamstrings is one of the main driving forces in sprint running.

The neuromuscular system has to be well coordinated to control these different hamstring functions in such a fast movement as sprinting, and if the hamstrings are not sufficiently strong and flexible they will be unable to meet this demand and the chances of hamstring strain increase. A complication that can place extra strain on the hamstrings is that during sprinting the trunk must remain upright and stable. The stabilising muscles of the stomach, low back and the gluteals should perform this role; however, if the core strength is not as good as it should be, the hamstrings will also have to stabilise the trunk, thus placing even more strain on them. If you want to avoid hamstring strains from sprinting, you need both strong hamstrings and strong core muscles - namely the gluteals, low back and abdominals.

Good core strength will also ensure that during each ground contact phase the pelvis remains level and lifted up, which allows greater power from the legs to be converted into horizontal speed. It will also reduce the risk of low-back injuries which are quite common in sprinters. Generally speaking, to help reduce risks of muscle strains and tendinitis type injuries in sprinting, athletes need to ensure they have very good range of motion in the all the leg muscles and joints. This takes the strain out of this very dynamic movement.

Importantly, though, sprinters should focus on dynamic flexibility training, to ensure that the flexibility they possess can be achieved actively throughout the whole range of motion. Research has shown that when there is a large gap between active and passive range of movement, injury risks are increased. (Active range of movement is a result of the athlete's own muscles, whereas passive range of movement is a result of an external stretching force.)

Injury prevention strategies

The first step for a sprinter who wants to avoid injury is to ensure full flexibility in all muscles with a regular stretching routine. In addition, part of each workout (often as an extended warm up) should be devoted to dynamic flexibility exercises. These dynamic flex exercises should focus particularly on ankle flexion and extension and hip flexion and extension range of movements. Most sprinters and their coaches know a whole set of these exercises.

The second step in injury prevention is to develop very good functional strength, including core stabilisation skills. Follow the suggested exercises for core stability above to ensure good recruitment of the transversus, gluteals and low-back muscles. Once these exercises have been mastered, more advanced core strength exercises can be used such as gluteal leg raises and back extensions on a Swiss ball, straight-legged dead lifts with a barbell, as well as the usual crunch type abdominal exercises.

When choosing strength exercises for the legs, always go for free weight, multi-joint exercises ahead of machines. If the muscles are not trained to work together in a coordinated fashion then the benefits for injury prevention are dramatically reduced. Exercises such as leg extensions for the quadriceps and leg curls for the hamstrings are probably quite useless as these are not movements involved in sprinting. Squats, dead lifts and power cleans should be the main choices for the legs. Ensure you learn correct techniques before moving on to big weights since poor lifting can affect the low back.

The following hamstring exercise progression is one of the best for sprinters.

Hamstring buck lifts

Lie on your back with your legs slightly bent and your feet up on a bench so your hips are flexed about 30 deg. Place the soles of your feet (not your heels) in contact with the bench.

Pushing down into the bench with your feet - and thereby recruiting the hamstrings - lift your hips off the floor until your back is fully extended. Complete three sets of 15 reps.

Once this exercise is comfortable, progress to the buck lifts with one leg. When this in turn becomes comfortable, progress to doing the buck lifts on one leg on a Swiss ball.

The pull of the hamstrings from the foot, extending the hip in the buck lift exercise is exactly the same as the pull of the hamstrings during ground contact in sprint running, making it totally functional in relation to sprinting. Once you can get to the Swiss ball level of the buck lift exercise, your hamstrings will be in great shape for sprinting.

SHOULDER EXERCISES AVOID SHOULDER PAIN

1. Balance your upper body workouts

A good way to avoid shoulder injuries is to make sure your upper body strength sessions are balanced. This means that every push or press exercise must be balanced with a pull or row exercise. Too many athletes and weight trainers focus on developing the 'mirror muscles', the upper trapezius, anterior deltoid and pectorals. As a consequence, the 'non-mirror muscles', lower trapezius, rhomboids, latissimus dorsi and rear deltoid, are underdeveloped. This leads to a muscular imbalance about the shoulder, which results in poor scapular stabilisation. since the non-mirror muscles are the ones that work to stabilise the scapula. In addition, over-developed mirror muscles can lead to a round-shouldered posture, which incorrectly places the scapula up and forward. Redressing this imbalance is very important for the prevention and rehabilitation of shoulder impingement injuries

The following is an example of a balanced upper body workout. Note the 1:1 ratio between push/press and pull/row exercises

— Bench press (pectorals, anterior deltoid)

— Seated row (rhomboids, mid trapezius, latissimus)

— Flies (pectorals)

— Rear lying prone flies (rhomboids, mid trapezius, rear deltoid)

— Lat raises (anterior mid deltoid, upper trapezius)

— Lat pull downs wide grip (latissimus, lower trapezius)

2. Limit your range of movement, and take it easy

Rehabilitation from a shoulder impingement injury should focus on rotator-cuff strengthening. However, it's important to remember that when it comes to re-introducing your weight training exercises, you must progress slowly. Often this means avoiding certain ranges of motion where the shoulder joint sub-acromial space is compressed the most. The impingement zone to avoid is between 70 and 120 degrees of shoulder abduction (when you move the arm laterally away from the side of the body)

To start training the non-mirror muscles, begin with the seated row, because the shoulder joint is not abducted in this exercise. Once the pain is completely gone, then introduce the overhead exercises such as pull ups and lat pull downs. You should be even more careful when it comes to the mirror-muscle exercises. However, incline bench press with arm abducted to 45 degrees would be a good choice to start again. Slowly build up to the normal bench-press range as strength improves.

It is also important that you don't increase your weights too soon. Remember that the ligaments and tendons have to adapt to exercise as well as the muscles, and they may take longer to do so. In the 12-20-rep range for a time before pushing up the weights, especially with the mirror-muscle exercises. Reducing your reps by two every two weeks is a good guideline. During heavy workouts, ensure that you warm up the shoulder joint and rotator cuff thoroughly prior to lifting.

3. Correct scapula positioning when performing exercises

The correct position for the scapula (shoulder blade) is back and rotated down. Essentially, this means maintaining a good 'military posture', with shoulders back and chest out. A round-shouldered or hunched posture is to be avoided at all times. To achieve the correct position, you need to use your rhomboids, mid and lower trapezius muscles to retract the shoulder and pull the scapula down.

When you perform any upper body weight training exercise, always get into the habit of starting with good upper body posture and pinching the shoulder blades together. You should feel that the scapula is a solid platform which keeps the shoulder correctly positioned while you perform the exercise. As mentioned last issue, a good way to learn the correct position is during the seated row exercise by keeping your scapula back and down while you move your arms. During the exercise, you should feel that the rhomboids and trapezius muscles are statically contracting to hold the scapula in place, and the latissimus is working to perform the movement.

Once you have the feel for maintained scapula stability during the seated row, try to achieve it during all upper-body exercises. What you might find is that exercises such as the press up or front raise, where the shoulder may become impinged, will not be painful if you stabilise your scapula correctly. In effect, by using the scapular muscles you can achieve better shoulder mechanics and avoid injury

Correct scapular stability is difficult to learn and demands a great deal of practice and concentration during your training sessions. You first need to understand what the correct position is, and often this requires a trainer/physio to guide you. Then, during training sessions, instruction and observation from a trainer can help you achieve and maintain the correct shoulder position.

4. Sports specific exercises - plyometrics for the shoulder

Just as rehabilitation training for leg injuries requires a functional progression from simple strength exercises to sports specific exercises, so does rehab for the shoulder. This means that for the athlete, eg, a thrower or tennis player, conventional resistance exercises in the gym may not be enough to allow a full return to competition. Often what is needed to bridge the gap are plyometric exercises for the shoulder that mimic sports specific movements.

Plyometrics Exercises

Plyometric exercises have two advantages. First, they are performed fast, and, second, they involve stretch-shortening-cycle movement patterns. This means they are much more sports-specific than conventional resistance exercises. In particular, plyometric exercises for the rear-shoulder and external rotator muscles are very useful because they provide eccentric training for these muscles.

This improves their ability to control the shoulder during the powerful concentric actions of the pectorals and anterior deltoid involved in throwing or serving. Thus it's important to ensure that your plyometric workouts are balanced between the prime movers (pectorals, latissimus, anterior deltoid) and the rear-shoulder and upper-back muscles.

Here are two suggestions. The key to both these exercises is that the medicine ball is caught, the impact quickly absorbed (fast eccentric phase) and then thrown back explosively (powerful concentric phase).

1. Power Drops (pectorals, anterior deltoids)

This exercise is like a plyometric bench press, using a medicine ball instead of a barbell. Lie on your back, legs bent and lower-back flat down. Partner stands above your head and drops ball (3-6kg). You catch ball with straight arms and then quickly let the ball drop to your chest, flexing your arms, and then immediately throw the ball back, powerfully extending your arms. Make sure you keep your back flat down, concentrating your effort on your arms only. Perform sets of 8-12 reps

2. Catch and throw backhands (external rotators)

This exercise is a plyometric version of the external rotator exercise described by Dr Kemp in the last issue, and is similar to a backhand shot in tennis. Stand with your feet shoulder-width apart, with a stable base and good posture. Bend your arm to 90 degrees and tuck your elbow into your side. Keeping your trunk facing forward, rotate your arm out ready to catch. Your partner stands to your right and throws a small ball (1kg) to your hand. You catch it, then quickly take the ball back across your body, rotating your arm inwards, and then immediately throw the ball back, powerfully rotating your arm out.

Make sure you don't use your trunk, and keep your elbow tucked into your side at all times, concentrating the effort on your rear shoulder and external rotator muscles. Repeat for the left side. Perform sets of 12-20 reps.

Rehabilitation process - so what exactly is the coach meant to do during the rehabilitation period? Here are a few pointers.

Exercise is a vital part of the rehabilitation process for most sporting injuries. The idea that an athlete is completely cured once the treatments on the therapist's couch are over is simply outdated. Instead, when athletes visit physios, in conjunction with receiving a course of treatment, they will be set specific strengthening and flexibility exercises. Exercises are included in rehabilitation programmes to ensure the injury site returns to a fully functional state and/or to ensure that the original cause of the injury is eliminated.

For example, an athlete recovering from tennis elbow will need to strengthen the wrist extensor muscles to prevent the injury recurring. The extensor muscles are often weak compared to the wrist flexor muscles and so are susceptible to overload. Or, an athlete recovering from a hamstring strain would need to stretch and strengthen the injured hamstring to ensure that flexibility and strength are equal for both injured and non-injured sides.

Because exercise is intrinsic to the rehabilitation process, trainers and coaches need to be aware that they have a significant part to play in helping their athletes back to full fitness. This article will discuss each stage of the injury management process in the hope of providing a few useful pointers for coaches and trainers.

First aid

If the athlete suffers an 'accident'-type injury, eg, a pulled hamstring or a sprained ankle, the trainer can help by carrying out the correct first-aid procedures. The familiar RICE protocol should always be followed: REST the injured part immediately; ICE the injury site; COMPRESS the injured site with strapping, and ELEVATE the injured limb. This protocol helps with pain relief and to control the inflammation and swelling. If it is done quickly, it can speed up healing time. For more serious injuries or bone fractures, eg, a broken leg, only those with proper training should attempt first-aid treatments. In serious cases, try to get professional help as quickly as possible.

If the injury is a 'chronic' type, eg, shin splints or tennis elbow, then it has occurred because the injured site has been overloaded during the athlete's exercise programme. The trainer must respond to the athlete immediately and stop the training to prevent any further damage. Remember, the quicker the athlete stops, the quicker the athlete recovers.

Diagnosis and treatment

The next step in injury management is getting an accurate diagnosis. The trainer needs to know where to take the athlete for expert help. In my experience, this is often where an athlete can come unstuck, as they can receive an inaccurate diagnosis and thus waste time following an inappropriate treatment plan. Only use your GP to refer you on to a sports-injury specialist because GPs are rarely experts in sports medicine unless they have a personal interest. Often the best people to see are physiotherapists specialising in sports injuries since they deal with such injuries on a regular basis. Even orthopaedic surgeons are not always sports-injury specialists, often spending most of their time with more general patients.

The sports-injury specialist will then plan and implement the treatment required. Usually, the initial stage of treatment involves reducing pain and promoting healing. As the trainer, you need to question the practitioner so you are aware of what is being done and why. Once pain and any swelling are reduced, the treatment will begin to involve more exercises. At this point, the physio will set exercises to target specific goals that will help solve the athlete's problems. Initially, this is likely to be mobility and flexibility training and then, later, strengthening work. This is where the athlete and trainer can work together.

Alternative Training

Athletes can continue to train even when they are injured. It means adopting different types of training or training methods that do not stress the injury. One of the major goals of the rehabilitation process is to maintain aerobic fitness levels by using alternative training methods. For instance, instead of running, athletes can try water running with a flotation belt, or cycling. As the coach, you should implement this alternative aerobic training programme as soon as possible. It is vital that athletes believe that even though they are injured, they can stay in shape.

In addition to maintaining aerobic fitness, the athlete can use the injury period as an opportunity to strengthen other areas of the body. Remember, it is only the injured part that needs to be rested, not the whole body. For example, a footballer with a groin strain can use the injury period to improve leg, trunk and upper-body strength. It's up to the coach to set an appropriate, and safe, strength programme.

Progressive Return to Full Training

Once the pain has subsided and the athlete has started to

meet the flexibility and strengthening goals, the physiotherapist will be able to advise on when normal training can start again. This is the point when clear communication between therapist, coach and athlete is vital. One of the major reasons why athletes suffer a recurrence of an injury is that they have started training too hard, too soon. What they fail to understand is that, just because the injured part is pain-free, it doesn't mean they are fully fit.

Once the athlete is able to use the injured part, he or she must gradually retrain the endurance, strength and coordination of that part so that it can withstand full competition conditions again. Thus, the goal at this stage in the rehabilitation process has moved on from healing the injury to regaining full function. To achieve this, the rehabilitation programme must be specific to the athlete's sport. For example, for the injured footballer, strength exercises should be functionally related movements, such as single-legged squats, jumps and plyometric drills.

The programme must also include proprio-ceptive training. This is very important because, in basic terms, proprioception is the coordination of balance and joint positioning sense. The brain must know accurately which position the joints are in so that movements can occur smoothly and effectively. Often, after a period of injury, especially joint injuries, the athlete can lose this ability. Any deficiency in this area, unless retrained, is likely to cause a recurrence of the injury. Therefore, exercises such as hopping on a trampette, unilateral balance drills, wobble-board exercises and hopping and jumping drills are important to retrain any lost proprioception. As well as being sports-specific, the rehabilitation programme must be progressive - for example, starting at 10 minutes running three times a week and then building slowly to 30 minutes running five times a week.

The final stage

A good example of the necessity for this final stage of the rehabilitation process is a footballer recovering from a hamstring injury. The player has completed a successful treatment period and the hamstrings' flexibility is equal both sides, as is their strength on the hamstrings curl station. The player can now jog pain-free. However, when he tried to join in a game, his hamstring felt weak. It is at this point that the player needs to slowly build up the training and include more specific exercises to bridge the gap between healing the injured part and making the injured part fully functional.

To do this, the player must gradually increase the amount of running he can do, as well as slowly increasing the speed he can run at. First, he must start with half-pace sprints, then three-quarter pace, until gradually increasing to full efforts. The player also needs to include more closed-chain multi-joint strength exercises, such as squats or dead lifts, where the hamstrings work in conjunction with other muscles.

He will also need to include dynamic and eccentric hamstring exercises, because this is how the hamstrings must work hard during sprinting. Both these types of exercises will strengthen the hamstrings in a sports-specific fashion. The player will also need to introduce kicking, ball-skills work and agility drills into his training, first at three-quarter speed and then full-out. This will ensure that all the skilled movements involved in the sport will have been slowly retrained.

After a period of this specific training and progression, the athlete will be ready to try playing a game. Once again, even this should be built up gradually, and the rehabilitation programme will need to be continued to ensure the problems do not recur. During this final stage, it is the coach's job to make sure the therapist is giving the athlete the right kind of rehabilitation programme, and also to make sure that the athlete continues to follow the programme set. The athlete cannot do too much but, at the same time, if he/she does too little then there will be no improvement in the areas that need to be worked on. This is where the coach must be fully involved, communicating with the therapist, and supervising the athlete. During this period the coach needs to invest as much time in the athlete, if not more, than in normal training.

Rotator Cuff Muscles Strengthening Exercises

Chronic shoulder pain is a common consequence of repetitive overhead activity, such as serving and smashing in tennis, freestyle or butterfly swimming, javelin throwing, or bowling in cricket. Usually such pain is a result of damage to the rotator cuff muscles. The rotator cuff group consists of four muscles, subscapularis, teres minor, infraspinatus and supraspinatus, which are positioned around the shoulder joint. These muscles are small, but their function is very important. Specifically, they act to keep the shoulder joint stable during movements of the arm by, in layman's terms, keeping the 'ball' in the 'socket'. There are three classic exercises for strengthening the rotator cuff: these are the lateral raise with internal rotation, the internal rotation exercise and the external rotation exercise, which can all be performed using a resistance band or dumbbells.

The lateral raise with internal rotation (LRIR) involves standing on the band with hands by your sides holding the end of the band in each hand, or standing holding dumbbells in each hand. The movement involves internally rotating your arms so that your thumbs point downwards, and then raising your arms out to the side until your elbows are just below the shoulder, keeping your thumbs pointing down as you raise. It is as if you are emptying a can of drink on the floor. This exercise is very popular, and is commonly recommended as part of a shoulder-injury rehabilitation programme.

The LRIR is specifically thought to train the supraspinatus, as this muscle is positioned above the shoulder joint and should be involved during arm abduction movements (lifting the arm out to the side). In fact, researchers Jobe and Moynes in 1982 claimed it was the most effective exercise for the supraspinatus. A variation of the LRIR exercise is to perform the arm abduction movement while lying on one's side.

This exercise has been advocated in a recent study by Joseph Horrigan, a chiropractor in Los Angeles, who has observed good clinical results for the treatment of rotator cuff problems with the use of the side lying abduction (SLA) exercise. Horrigan states that the exercise should be performed while lying on one side and holding a dumbbell with your palm facing into your leg. You then raise your arm straight up to an angle of 45 degrees. He recommends that men use a dumbbell weighted to 8% of body weight and women use 5% of body weight.

Horrigan and his study team decided to examine the muscle activity of the SLA and compare it with the activity of the LRIR, to determine if there is any advantage in using one exercise over the other. To do this they used a slightly uncommon method of measuring muscle activity, Magnetic Resonance Imaging (MRI). MRI scans are used routinely as diagnostic tools for examining injuries, but less regularly used in other areas of sports science.

The reason MRI can be used to measure muscle activity is that the signal intensity of the muscle image increases after it has been exercised. This is known as an exercise-induced enhancement. Thus, by comparing MRI scans before and after a particular exercise, researchers can tell which muscles have been active. More importantly, MRI can also quantify the amount of muscle activity involved in the exercise by analysing the strength of the signal intensity. The bigger the change in signal intensity between before and after the exercise, then the more the muscle has been working.

Comparisons with EMG analysis, which is the more traditional method for measuring muscle activity, has shown that the MRI is a very sound method. In fact, one could argue that it is superior since it is easy to compare different muscle groups or different exercises by simply comparing the percentage change in signal intensity. For example, if one performed an exercise and the signal intensity in the biceps muscle increased 69% whereas the signal intensity in the triceps muscle increased only 5%, one could confidently conclude that the exercise works the biceps much more than the triceps.

Horrigan and his team used this type of comparison in their experiment. They measured the signal intensity of the trapezius, deltoid, supraspinatus, subscapularis, infraspinatus and teres minor before and after three different shoulder exercises, the LRIR, the SLA and the traditional military press exercise (MP). Five subjects were used and all had no shoulder problems.

The supraspinatus, subscapularis and infraspinatus muscles are all most active during the SLA exercise compared to the other two. This supports Horrigan's observation that it is a very effective rotator cuff exercise. The SLA produces no activity in teres minor, the fourth rotator cuff muscle, but neither LRIR and MP produce very much either. Teres minor is situated behind the shoulder and acts as a lateral rotator, and perhaps requires a specific lateral rotation exercise to be active.

The deltoid is also most active during the SLA, suggesting that it is a very effective shoulder exercise in general, not just for the rotator cuff. Interestingly, the SLA involves much less trapezius activity than the LRIR and MP, presumably because the exercise is performed lying down and so there is less shoulder elevation. This reduction in trapezius activity is not necessarily a disadvantage because the trapezius is often strong, especially in the upper fibres, and can be too dominant. This muscle imbalance can contribute to a hunched and rounded shoulder posture during shoulder movements which can exasperate shoulder injuries.

The SLA is also ideal in that it only involves 45 degrees of abduction, compared to the LRIR which involves almost 90 deg. When the arm is abducted between 70 deg and 120 degrees the sub-acromial space, which is the area within the shoulder joint, is compressed. This can cause impingement of the soft tissue within that joint space, which can lead to pain or injuries. Therefore, as well as being more effective, the SLA also seems to be a safer exercise than the LRIR.

Groin Injuries Treatment Exercises

Immediate management

Immediate icing of direct muscle tears of the groin and especially adductor attachment tears is beneficial and necessary in the 24-hour period after the injury. Unlike hamstring injuries, however, movement while icing is not necessary and may in fact be detrimental to the turn-around time of adductor injuries. This will be expanded further in the section on stretching.

Soft-tissue therapy

Any therapy that reduces muscle tone in the adductor

muscles will be a useful adjunct in the treatment of this injury. This may be any soft-tissue massage (ischaemic pressure and longitudinal flush) in the area below the tear or 'trigger point' injection therapy into the adductor muscle belly.

Groin Straps

It is common practice in Australia (particularly the Rugby League haven of New South Wales) to use groin straps in the management of adductor lesions. However, they are almost unheard of in the United Kingdom.

The rationale behind the adductor (groin) strap is similar to the Chopart or patella tendon strap. The application of the strap directs force on to the strap and away from the injured tissue. In relation to the adductors, the strap is usually applied high up around the thigh as close to the adductor tubercle as possible. It is placed on quite tight to be supportive but not occlusive to the femoral artery, vein and nerves. This then takes stress away from the adductor tubercle. It will result in an immediate decrease (not abolition) in pain on functional movement and adductor squeeze testing.

The athlete is instructed to keep the strap in situ 24/7, except for showering and sleeping (however, there is no reason why it needs to be removed during sleep). The athlete can continue to wear the strap during rehabilitation and return to sport.

Stretching

For some bizarre reason, the adductor muscles are the only muscles that respond POORLY to stretching in the initial post-injury period. There is no plausible explanation for this phenomenon. One possible reason (and this reason does have its flaws) is that the adductor muscle does not operate through a large range of motion during the execution of most sporting manoeuvres. Therefore, stretching of the muscle into end-of-range positions in the initial period may in fact place the muscle in a position it is not used to and comfortable with. This may lead to an adverse tissue reaction that further adds to the stress of the muscle and results in further increases in muscle tone.

The alternative to stretching the adductor muscle group is to use 'isometric stretching'. This is done by squeezing a football, rugby ball or netball. The ball is placed between the knees in the three testing positions mentioned on page 11 of the last issue of SIB. The ball is then squeezed to the point of discomfort but not pain. The contraction is held for 10 seconds and the legs are then moved up to the next position, 45-degrees knee flexion. Again, this is held for 10 seconds and the legs are then lifted to the 90-degree hip flexion position and contraction repeated for 10 seconds. Back down to legs straight and start again. This can be done five times in each position.

The theory behind isometric stretching of the adductors is as follows. As the muscle isometrically contracts against a stationary and non-deformable object (the ball), the muscle tissue will undergo a degree of shortening. As a consequence, the tendon attached proximally to the muscle will be required to elongate slightly to keep the entire muscle-tendon complex at the same length. The amount of stretch and elongation we are talking is tiny; however, it is enough to cause a slight elongation in the tendon and tenoperiosteal junction. No other muscle in and around the pelvis responds in the same way to this technique as the adductor muscles.

Another way to isometrically stretch is to have the therapist control the weight of the leg, which is in knee extension. The leg is then lifted into progressive degrees of hip flexion, abduction and internal or external rotation.

The patient is then instructed to gently pull into the opposite direction (adduction, flexion and the other rotation). This is very similar to a PNF contract-relax stretch. The leg can then be lifted and placed into more progressive positions based on the feeling of movement blocks (a term those trained in 'muscle energy' will be familiar with). This can be continued into the extreme end-of-range positions of hip flexion, with moderate amounts of rotation and minimal range of abduction.

Strength Retraining

Initial strength retraining may take the form of 'adductor squeezing' as described above. This can be started almost at day one. The act of performing the adductor squeeze thus serves two functions; isometric stretch and strength retraining. This can be progressed from supine lying positions to wall squat positions. The protocol is the same: aim for 10-second holds and attempt five repetitions in each position. As adductor squeeze and function improves, the following exercises may be added to strengthen the adductor muscle:

— *Theraband adductions (crook lying):* lying supine with knees and hips bent to 45 degrees. Place theraband around knee and attach to leg of table. Let the leg fall out to position of abduction and contract back to knees together position. This can be progressed into greater range, greater speed and greater resistance.

— *Theraband adductions (standing)*: standing with theraband around heel, hold on to chair for support, allow band to pull leg into abduction, contract back to adduction. Perform with the foot in front of the stance leg and foot behind the stance leg. And very important, do both legs. The adductor needs to retrain its movement function as well as its stabilising function.

- *Lunging (around the clock)*: feet together, step out in front (12 o'clock) and take weight via a lunge action. Push back to start position. Step out to the side (3 or 9 o'clock position) and back, then step backwards (6 o'clock) and back. Again, do BOTH legs.
- *Lateral step ups*: place a knee-height box or chair about three feet at your side. Step up on to the box sideways and down again. Again do both legs. Progress by increasing speed.
- *Swiss ball squats*: on a Swiss ball, either stand (for the vertically challenged) or perform a partial squat. This is a great isometric-adductor strength exercise.
- *Weights*: this is not the time or the place to discuss weight-training routines, but a few key principles regarding leg weights need to be laid down. First, perform and be happy with two-legged bilateral exercises before progressing to one-leg unilateral exercises. For example, do two-legged leg press before attempting one-legged leg press. Second, be careful with the progression of load and speed. Adductors tend to work exponentially harder as one approaches the one-repetition maximums. Respect this before progressing loads. Furthermore, ballistic movements such as power cleans and snatches tend to recruit more adductor activity. Exercises where the feet do not leave the floor are generally safer initially.
- *Functional strengthening*: field activities such as side-stepping and cariocas.

Rehab running/training

This stage has similar progressions to the fitness testing mentioned below. In order to retrain the adductors for functional use, activities need to be presented in a logical and progressive order.

The stages can be progressed from one day to the next, or progressed within the same session depending on presentation of symptoms. The progressions are as follows:

— *Straight line running*: distances can be progressed in pyramid fashion. That is, 10m, 20m, 30m, 40m and so on. Overall maximum distance will depend on the individual athlete's requirements (sport and position). Speed needs to be progressed sensibly and always on the basis of presenting symptoms (pain) and clinical signs (adductor squeeze and palpation). Aim to reach full top-end speed before reaching flat-out acceleration and deceleration.

— *Weave running*: progressed as above but instead of in a straight line, the athlete runs curves.

— *Sideways shuttles*: stand on a line. Side-step five times to the right and then sprint forward 10 metres. Rapidly stop and then side-step five times to the left. Sprint 10 metres again and repeat the process to the right. This can continue for as many 10-metre segments as desired.

— *Sprint and cut*: sprint forward 20 metres and step rapidly to the left at a 45-degree angle. Walk back and repeat to the right.

— *Cone drills*: place five cones out in a random order over a 10-x-10- metre square. The idea of this drill is for the athlete to sprint to one cone, rapidly stop and reach down to touch the cone, look up at the tester who points at another cone for the athlete to sprint towards. This continues for 20 seconds and can be repeated as many times as desired.

— *Functional skills*: depending on the sport played, this would include (if relevant) kicking, scrums, tackling, jumping etc..

Fitness Testing

Those involved with the management of groin injuries (physiotherapists, sports medicine physicians, orthopods and athletic trainers) all have their favourite ways of assessing fitness for competition. Outlined below is a very direct and accurate method of assessing the functional ability to perform in competition and avoid risk of re-injury following an adductor-muscle strain.

The premise of the following fitness testing protocol is that two criteria must be satisfied; first, that the athlete can perform the testing procedure pain-free and without functional limitation, and second, that the adductor muscle does not 'tone up' two to three hours following fitness testing. This is assessed by palpation of the muscle. It is common for athletes to able to complete such a fitness testing session, and then have all sorts of problems in the few hours following.

As far as timing goes, this type of testing can be done the day before competition or even on the morning of an afternoon competition. This is in contrast to hamstring muscle injuries that ideally should be fitness tested 48 hours prior to competition.

Procedure

Assess adductor squeeze (pain and weakness) at three testing positions and feel muscle tone to gain an initial baseline. These should feel good if you have progressed to fitness testing.

Ten minutes of general running and stretching

Straight line running: 5 x 40 metre run-throughs progressed from warm-up speed to full speed. The rate of acceleration is not important at this point; the focus is on reaching full speed before 40 metres. Walk return after each repetition.

Straight line acceleration: (over 20 metres): 1 x 20 metre flying start (jog in before flat-out acceleration); 1 x 20 metre upright start (off the mark); 1 x 20 metre 3-point stance start; 1 x 20 metre starting on stomach.

Weave running: 4 x 40m: running in a 5-10 metre channel, the athlete sprints whilst weaving between two parallel lines (the in- goal area of a Rugby pitch is ideal). This is a pure weave (similar to running around a curve) and no side-stepping is involved. For example, the athlete may be instructed to touch the right line and then left line twice each on the first run, three times on the second, and so on. By increasing the number of touches on each line, the angles involved in the weave will become more acute and more challenging for the groin muscles.

Cutting manoeuvres: sprint 20 metres straight line and cut (stepping off) 45 degrees to the left or right (at full speed) and continue to sprint for another 10 metres before decelerating. Complete two to the left and two to the right.

Cone drills: place five cones out in a random order over a 10-x-10-metre square. The idea of this drill is for the athlete to sprint to one cone, rapidly stop and reach down to touch the cone, look up at the tester who points at another cone for the athlete to sprint towards. This continues for 20 seconds. The athlete repeats this for a total of four repetitions with one-minutes rest between efforts.

The final two efforts are modified in the following way. Instead of bending down to touch the cones, the athlete falls to the ground on his/her front. Before the athlete gets back to their feet, the assessor places some pressure on the athletes back so that they need to fight their way back on to their feet before continuing. This continues for 20 seconds (in this time expect the athlete to hit the ground 3-4 times). As a word of caution, this is very fatiguing to do at full speed for a full 20 seconds (if you disagree, try it yourself). Therefore, if testing on the morning of a game the time period may need to be modified depending on the individual fitness characteristics of the athlete/player.

Kicking: if this is a common skill component encountered in the game. Start with short-distance kicking and progress to long kicking and kicking across the body and kicking on the run. Warm down and stretch for 10 minutes.

Re-assess adductor squeeze and muscle tone: immediately after warm down, then again 2-3 hours following fitness testing. It is important that the adductor muscle is not treated in this time period.

The above testing procedure will assess the ability to perform all physical components required for competition whether the sport is football, rugby, basketball or Australian Rules Football. The distances can be modified for court sports such as tennis, basketball and netball, and the need to assess the ability to spring off the ground is not essential for these sorts of sports.

The above test should be performed pain-free and without functional limitation. Examples of functional limitation would be the inability or reluctance to turn away from the injured side, holding back on the acceleration component and obvious limping (hopefully the assessor would be wise enough to not even bother fitness testing in this situation).

The re-assessment of muscle tone is also of critical importance. If muscle tone is to increase following such an intense and involved testing session, then it will do so within the first two to three hours following the testing. From a pathological perspective, an increase in muscle tone is an indication that the original source of pathology (whether it be muscle or tenoperiosteal junction) has been irritated and has 'driven' the tone in the involved muscle belly. This is an important indication that the muscle is subject to possible further damage (in the form of a strain) especially under fatigue. The increase in tone will be quite obvious when you palpate if you have been assessing tone on a regular basis during preceding treatment days.

— Groin/Pelvic Pathologies
— Adductor muscle tears (Grade 1-3) (Add Brevis, Add Longus, Gracilis)
— Adductor Tendonitis/
— Tenoperiostitis
— Osteitis Pubis (Pubic Symphysitis)
— Inguinal/Sportsman's Hernia
— Posterior wall insufficiency
— Conjoined tendon tear
— Ilioinguinal nerve irritation
— Iliopsoas strain/bursitis
— Stress fracture (pubic ramus)
— Referred pain (lumbar spine and sacroiliac joint)
— Obturator nerve neuropathy
— Sinister pathologies such as prostatitis, UTIs, testicular tumour, infection.

Wrist Tendinitis and Wrist Injuries

The wrist is a complex structure that is particularly prone to injury in sports. Approximately a quarter of athletic injuries involve the wrist and hand. Some sports involve a higher risk of wrist injury than others. The overuse injuries that are common in the wrist include tendinitis, tenosynovitis, tunnel syndromes and stress fractures.

The wrist joint is formed proximally by the distal surface of the radius and ulna and the attached fibrocartillage disc, and distally by the scaphoid, lunate and triquetral bones. The wrist as a region extends from the distal radius and ulna to the base of the metacarpals. The wrist positions and supports the hand and therefore has to combine strength and precision with a wide range of movement with stability.

The position of the bones of the carpus is controlled both by their bony shape and their ligamentous support. Most of the musculotendinous units that power movement in the wrist traverse the carpal bones and insert in to the base of the metacarpals, therefore indirectly controlling the position of the carpal bones. The pisiform is a sesamoid bone within the tendon of flexor carpi ulnaris that then inserts distally into the hamate and the fifth metacarpal base. Extensor carpi radialis longus and brevis insert in to the dorsal base of the index and middle metacarpals respectively. Flexor carpi radialis inserts in to the volar base of the index and middle metacarpals and may send a slip to the scaphoid tubercle.

Stability

The wrist tendons are closely applied to the wrist bones and therefore act close to the centre of rotation of the joint. This mechanical disadvantage results in the generation of large tension in the wrist tendons to power wrist movement. Calculations of joint reaction forces in the wrist are complex but suggest a multiplication of the applied loads in the hand. It is estimated that the compressive loads at the carpometacarpal joint can reach ten times the force applied at the finger tips. The forces are transmitted through the articular surfaces of the wrist joint and supporting ligaments depending on the position of the joint.

The inherently unstable bony anatomy is controlled by the passive restraint of the complex intrinsic and extrinsic wrist ligaments that prevent collapse of the carpal bones. Failure of the bony structure, the joint surfaces or the ligaments causes collapse of the wrist. Any condition that affects the stability of the carpal bones or the normal function of the wrist tendons will therefore result in a marked reduction of grip strength.

The extensor tendons are held closely applied to the dorsal surface of the distal radius and ulna by the extensor retinaculum. This is a ribbon-like fascial band 2.5 cm wide that extends obliquely from the anterolateral surface of the radius across the dorsum of the wrist inserting in to the pisiform and triquetral bones, but not directly in to the ulna. The radius and carpus are free to rotate about the ulna without affecting tension in the extensor retinaculum. The extensor retinaculum prevents bowstringing of the extensor tendons with wrist extension, and bony attachments of the retinaculum produce six extensor compartments that control the tendons with wrist movement.

Common Sites for Pain

Pain arising from musculotendinous units in the wrist originates from their bony attachments or from where they pass through tight fascial tunnels lubricated by a synovial bursa. The four common sites for pain in the upper limb are the first dorsal compartment (De Quervain's tendovaginitis), digital flexors (trigger finger), flexor carpi radialis tendinitis, and lateral epicondylitis (tennis elbow). Sites for other wrist tendinities are comparatively less common, but can occur in the wrist extensors, intersection syndrome, extensor policis longus, extensor digiti minimi, and abnormal connections between the thumb and index flexors.

Epidemiological data from work-related injury suggests that the risk of wrist tendinitis in occupations involving forceful repetitive actions is up to 29 times that of non-forceful or non-repetitive jobs. Sporting activities that involve forceful repetitive overuse of the wrist have a high incidence of wrist tendinitis. It is not clear, however, what level of force and repetition causes wrist tendinitis, and there appears to be a complex interaction of many factors including gender, hormonal, neurogenic and mechanical factors in the aetiology of wrist tendinitis.

Management

Ergonomic considerations are paramount in the management of sports-related wrist tendinitis. They are equipment related, technique related, or a combination. Many of the advances in sport- equipment design are driven by the need to minimise the damaging forces on the wrist. For example, large racquet heads appear to have reduced the incidence of upper-limb injuries in tennis players.

Vibration is an important factor increasing the force required to grasp an object, decreasing the proprioreceptive input and reflexly increasing muscle contraction via a process termed the tonic vibration reflex. The threshold for motor unit recruitment is decreased by vibration, and the force of contraction is increased in the presence of vibration. Vibration also potentiates the force of contraction for subsequent contractions. The tonic vibration reflex can be decreased by cutaneous stimulation or acupuncture.

Tendons respond to increased stress by increasing collagen content and cross sectional area. If the adaptive capacity of the tendon is exceeded, the collagen bundles are damaged. Damaging forces can be single or repetitive. Collagen fibres appear to be damaged by repeated application of stress below the ultimate tensile strength of the collagen. Sex differences in the mechanical properties of tendon material have been demonstrated, with female flexor digitorum profundus tendons found to be stiffer and to exhibit less creep than male tendons.

Repair

The repair process following injury consists of inflammation, proliferation, and maturation. The inflammation phase, characterised by swelling warmth and oedema, continues until the damaging forces cease. Continued damaging forces cause chronic inflammation, secondary adhesion and degeneration. The term tendinosis refers to degeneration of the tendon without signs of associated inflammation. The lack of signs of acute inflammation in many of the lesions may be due to their chronic nature.

Narrowing of the fibrous tissue tunnels that enclose the tendons or swelling of the tendons increases the local pressure on the tendons. Synovitic reactions within the tendon sheaths further reduce the available space causing a local increase in pressure and pain. Tendon nodules may cause a block in the normal smooth passage of the tendon as in trigger finger, but true triggering is rare in wrist tendinitis.

Wrist Tendinitis Diagnosis and Wrist Tendinitis Treatment

The diagnosis and treatment of wrist tendinitis starts with a full history and physical examination. Important questions in the history include work and sporting activity, a history of previous upper-limb injury, penetrating trauma with foreign bodies, problems in the shoulder, elbow or wrist, exacerbating and relieving factors, and the functional impairment caused by the pain.

Systemic illnesses associated with tendinitis include diabetes, rheumatoid arthritis, crystal arthropathy, and connective tissue disorders. A chronic indolent infection can cause tenosynovitis and mimic benign tenosynovitis. Tumours in this region are rare, but can cause pain and loss of function, mimicking benign tenosynovitis.

Pain from wrist tendinitis is generally described as aching, provoked by exercise, and relieved by rest. Other pain patterns raise suspicions of an alternative diagnosis. Pain from an involved tendon is usually well located to that tendon, its tendon sheath or its bony insertion, making the clinical diagnosis clear. However, pain arising from the radio carpal, mid carpal or carpometacarpal joins causes pain on movement that may be reproduced by the provocative tests for each tendinitis condition. Plain radiographs are obtained to exclude underlying bone pathology, stress fractures or joint degeneration. Soft-tissue films including oblique views of the affected area may demonstrate calcification indicative of acute calcific tendinitis.

The treatment is generally rest, splintage, non-steroidal anti- inflammatory medication, and occasionally steroid injection, with surgery reserved for severe cases that don't respond to conservative treatment.

De Quervain's Tenosynovitis

This is the most common wrist tendinitis. It involves the first dorsal compartment of the wrist. This compartment contains the tendons of abductor policis longus (APL) and extensor policis brevis (EPB). Multiple tendon slips are present in 50% to 90% of specimens and the compartment is often subdivided. Failure of surgical treatment is often due to a lack of appreciation of these anatomic variants.

The clinical findings in de Quervain's tenosynovitis are of pain, swelling and tenderness over the first dorsal compartment, increased with thumb motion. Finklestein's test increases the pain on radial deviation of the wrist with the thumb in a neutral position.

Triggering of the thumb indicates nodule formation either in the long thumb flexor tendon or in the first dorsal compartment. This indicates a more extensive stenosing tenosynovitis often recalcitrant to conservative treatment. The condition is more common in women between 30 and 60 years of age, becomes bilateral in 30% of patients and is a particular problem with golfers.

The flexor carpi radialis (FCR) tendon runs in a sheath from it muscular origin to its insertion. It enters its own fibro-osseous tunnel at the wrist, occupying 90% of the tunnel volume. Swelling of the tendon, tendon sheath or arising from adjacent joints causes pressure on the FCR tendon. Pain is generally felt at the proximal border of the trapezium and is associated with wrist flexion. There may be a swelling of the entire tendon sheath or a localised bony constriction. This can be shown on plain radiographs (carpal tunnel views) or a CT scan. Primary tendinitis may respond to non- operative or injection treatment, but extrinsic causes often require surgical decompression.

Flexor carpi ulnaris (FCU) tendinitis is a common problem in racquet sports that involve repetitive forced wrist flexion. Pain can be felt along the FCU tendon, around the pisiform or its distal insertion. Pain may arise from arthrosis of the pisotriquetral joint or instability of the pisiform.

Drummer Boy Palsy

Extensor policis longus tendinitis is also known as *drummer boy palsy*. There is usually a predisposing cause found in the history such as direct trauma, or an undisplaced wrist fracture. Rupture or tendinitis usually occurs within 8 weeks of injury, but can occur many years later.

Extensor indicis proprius (EIP) tendinitis and extensor digiti minimi tendinitis are rare conditions. EIP tendinitis is associated with a muscle belly within the tendon sheath in 75% of cases.

Intersection syndrome occurs where the tendons of extensor policis brevis (EPB) and abductor policis longus (APL) cross extensor carpi radialis longus (ECRL) and brevis (ECRB), between 4 and 8 cm proximal to the wrist. Inflammation of the intervening bursa causes crepitation that is palpable and sometimes audible. Intersection syndrome is a particular problem in rowers and weight lifters. Non-operative management is generally successful, but for recalcitrant cases operative treatment including release of constrictive fascia and excision of the inflamed bursa may be required.

Restrictive thumb index tenosynovitis termed Linberg's syndrome is rarely a problem in athletes. It results from straining a connection between the flexor policis longus and index flexor digitorum profundus tendons that is present in 31% of the population. Symptoms are caused by attempted thumb flexion with the index finger extended. This results in pain in the distal radial volar forearm. The treatment is generally avoidance of the precipitating action with surgery rarely required.

Tennis Elbow Treatments and Exercises

Between 10 and 50 per cent of players suffer from tennis elbow. Here's what science says about tennis elbow treatments and preventing tennis elbow. Wimbledon may be only a distant memory, but the dubious charms of lateral epicondylitis, or tennis elbow, remain ever present for those who suffer from it. What are the latest treatments and exercises for dealing with this minor scourge?

Before seeking to eradicate the symptoms, you first need to be aware of the tissues you have injured. The elbow is a hinge joint, allowing both flexion and extension. Functional stability in your elbow is gained through its bony anatomy and its ligaments. We are purely concerned with the lateral (outside) aspect of the elbow. Tennis elbow involves injury to the extensor muscles of your forearm and its tendinous origin.

There is more than one joint involved in movements at your elbow. The joint utilises three articulations (how the three bones of the arm move against each other) to allow movement at the elbow joint. The three bones in question are the humerus (upper arm) and the radius and ulna (bones of the forearm). The radio-ulnar joint is most crucial in this injury as it plays a role in pronation (turning the palm of your hand towards the floor) and supination (turning the palm of your hand away from the floor.

The humerus's two condyles (found at the far end of the humerus) give articulating surfaces at your elbow joint. Above the condyles are the medial and lateral epicondyles. It is the lateral epicondyle where you will find the origin for the extensor-supinator group (forearm muscles that provide extension and supination). Your forearm extensor muscles are in action during wrist extension and are particularly important in the backhand stroke. Tennis involves repeated gripping and twisting movements, which work your extensor muscles.

Tennis elbow injuries mostly occur if repetitive micro-trauma is placed on the tissues in question. The micro-trauma involves forces that the tissues are unable to cope with. These forces can be worsened by several predisposing factors. If you buy a new racket or use one with strings that are too taut or with a handle that is too large, you could be putting yourself at risk. In addition, if you suddenly increase your playing intensity coupled with a poor technique - essentially the backhand - you reduce your body's ability to withstand these forces.

There are many factors that can lead to tennis elbow:

1 If the amount of external rotation in your shoulder is restricted, it can lead to extra strain being placed on the elbow
2 An overuse injury during wrist extension can occur if your extensor carpi radialis brevis (forearm muscle involved in wrist extension) takes on the role of flexing the elbow ahead of the biceps
3 A lack of mobility in your back
4 Poor flexibility
5 Playing surfaces: harder ones mean increased forces

Faults in technique can also contribute. A comparative study using tennis elbow sufferers and a non-symptomatic control group revealed several differences. Sufferers showed poor body positioning and greater involvement of their forearm extensor muscles. They also showed rapid change from wrist flexion to wrist extension when striking the ball and early in the follow-through. This placed the wrist in an unstable position to withstand repeated forces. Importantly, the backhand stroke heightened these differences.

Tennis Elbow Treatments

If you are suffering from tennis elbow, you will most likely have pain radiating down the lateral side of your elbow or stiffness in this area. Your symptoms may disappear if you stop playing, but this is obviously self-defeating. Other primary treatments can include anti-inflammatory drugs (NSAIDs), injections, and by following the RICE (rest, ice, compression and elevation) method. These, however, merely treat the symptoms and don't address the underlying factors that caused the injury.

Noteboom categorises five stages of treatments for tennis elbow:

1. Reduce pain
2. Reduce inflammation
3. Induce the healing process
4. Maintain fitness
5. Control force placed on injured tissues.

To follow the latter, of course, you must first get an accurate diagnosis, pinpointing the injured tissues. Physiotherapy is needed, both for this and to explain how to reduce the contributory forces being placed on your elbow.

Tennis Elbow Exercises and Rehabilitation

Stretching your forearm extensors is important in establishing a full range of motion and in achieving alignment during tissue repair. Begin your first stretch by extending your arm with the palm of your hand facing downwards and then pull your hand upwards towards your forearm. The second stretch is a reversal of this, meaning that you pull your hand downwards towards the underside of your forearm. If this stretch proves painful, simply keep your arm bent during the stretch to reduce the intensity.

As you begin to show signs of improvement, resistance exercises can be added. The weight should be light at first, perhaps with dynabands being used before progressing to dumbbells. Wrist curls are a good exercise that works the underside of the forearm muscles. Grasp a dumbbell in each hand and sit down. Then lay your forearms on your thighs with your hands dangling over your knees, your palms facing upwards. Begin your first repetition by curling the weight upwards at the wrist and then slowly lowering. A similar exercise to work the tops of your forearms can be performed by starting with your palms facing downwards. Initially, three sets of 10 repetitions should be performed daily; once you achieve 25 reps, add an extra two-kilogram weight.

You could also include isometric exercises. The first requires you to squeeze a tennis ball in the palm of your hand and hold it momentarily before releasing. The second is a rubber band exercise, where the band should be placed at your fingertips. Start the exercise by extending your fingers outwards and then hold for a few seconds before releasing. Aim to perform these exercises twice a day.

Once your overall strength improves, other elbow extension exercises can be included where appropriate. The important point is to maintain your aerobic fitness by cycling, say, or jogging - any exercise that doesn't strain the elbow. This will help smooth your transition back on to the tennis court.

Tennis Elbow Cures

There's a good reason that most amateur racket sport players are familiar with the term - tennis elbow. The fact is that most players with less than perfect technique struggle with tennis elbow as a direct consequence of poor form when hitting the ball.

To reduce the threat of tennis elbow, there are number of exercises you can do and measures you can take. But they won't help you if you already have it. So it's of primary importance to figure out exactly which type of tennis elbow you have. That's right, there's more than one.

Types of Elbow Problem

Elbow problems can be classified as either 'backhand tennis elbow' or 'forehand tennis elbow'. Backhand elbow is usually caused by lack of strength in the extensor muscles of the forearm (the muscles which attach on the outer side of the elbow) and/or by poor technique. For example, if a player hits backhand shots by leading with the elbow, the head of the racket lags behind the elbow during the initial part of the stroke. Just before impact with the ball, the racket must accelerate dramatically, travelling much faster than the elbow. When the racket actually hits the ball, the impact forces the racket to slow down immediately, and the heavy force of impact is transmitted directly to the elbow. One remedy for this is to hit the backstroke with the entire arm - instead of 'snapping' the forearm ahead at the elbow joint

Forehand tennis elbow is less common among novice players, primarily because the average tennis participant's inside-elbow muscles are stronger than the outside-elbow ones. However, professional players are at high risk for the malady, because their attempts to put spin on the ball (for topspin forehands and spin serves) lead to excessive action at the wrist, which in turn strains the elbow on the inside.

To limit your risk of tennis elbow, the following steps should be very helpful:

— Work with a knowledgeable coach to improve your technique.

— Make sure that the grip on your racket is the right size for you (a grip that is too large or too small increases wrist-muscle fatigue, making the wrist unstable and leading to too-large forces at the elbow)

— Play on clay or grass courts (cement and other hard courts raise ball velocity, producing greater impacts and higher elbow forces)

— Use less-stiff rackets (the stiffer the racket, the larger the force transmitted to the arm)

— String your racket less tightly (the tighter the strings, the higher the force)

— Strength train your wrist muscles, as well as the muscles on the inside and outside of the elbow. For the wrists, good exercises include squeezing a tennis ball and doing wrist curls and extensions with a dumbbell

— Carry out stretching exercises for the wrist muscles and muscles on the outside and inside of the elbow after you play, or after a warm-up which includes light hitting of the ball

— Avoid playing more than four times a week, and if soreness appears after a game, don't play again until the pain disappears

Treating Elbow Tendonitis

For many amateur racket-sport athletes, elbow tendonitis or 'tennis-elbow' is an all too frequent injury – often resulting in stiffness, soreness, and outright pain. Basically, elbow tendonitis is an overuse injury caused by repeated contractions of muscles connected to the elbow joint of the arm used to hit the ball. Stress on the elbow is inevitable, because some of the force created when the ball hits the racket automatically passes from the racket into the forearm and then to the elbow. This repeated impact produces trauma to the tissues surrounding the elbow, leading to inflammation and soreness.

Elbow tendonitis can be classified as either 'backhand tennis elbow' or 'forehand tennis elbow'. Backhand elbow is usually caused by lack of strength in the extensor muscles of the forearm (the muscles which attach on the outer side of the elbow) and/or by poor technique, hence why amateur players are the worse sufferers of the condition.

Forehand tennis elbow is less common among novice players, primarily because the average tennis participant's inside-elbow muscles are stronger than the outside-elbow ones. However, professional players are at high risk for the malady, because their attempts to put spin on the ball (for topspin forehands and spin serves) lead to excessive action at the wrist, which in turn strains the elbow on the inside

The frequency of elbow tendonitis increases with age and the number of years of play. Sadly for veterans, it takes longer to correct in older players too also. To limit your risk of tennis elbow, the following steps should be very helpful:

- Work with a knowledgeable coach to improve your technique
- Make sure that the grip on your racket is the right size for you (a grip that is too large or too small increases wrist-muscle fatigue, making the wrist unstable and leading to too-large forces at the elbow)
- Play on clay or grass courts (cement and other hard courts raise ball velocity, producing greater impacts and higher elbow forces)
- Use less-stiff rackets (the stiffer the racket, the larger the force transmitted to the arm)
- String your racket less tightly (the tighter the strings, the higher the force)
- Strength train your wrist muscles, as well as the muscles on the inside and outside of the elbow. For the wrists, good exercises include squeezing a tennis ball and doing wrist curls and extensions with a **dumbbell**

— Carry out stretching exercises for the wrist muscles and muscles on the outside and inside of the elbow after you play, or after a warm-up which includes light hitting of the ball

— Avoid playing more than four times a week, and if soreness appears after a game, don't play again until the pain disappears.

8

Tennis Nutrition

A player's overall dietary needs on and off the court are typically pretty straightforward. Unfortunately, some players will focus on trying the latest fad in nutritional supplements, using the rationale "*this* must be what I'm missing!" With all of this information, nutrition for tennis can become more than a little confusing. Dietary strategies should be adjusted for such factors as a player's age, fitness, level of competition, intensity of play, environment, time of competition, duration of play, amount of time between matches, as well as many others.

From a nutritional standpoint, preparing for a tournament match is further challenged by the unpredictability of getting on the court; a match that is supposed to start at 11 a.m. may not actually begin until 1:30. This raises questions like, "Should that player now have lunch or not?" and "What types of foods should the player consume during the delay to remain 'peaked' for competition?"

Energy Balance and Fuel for the Body

Players can readily expend a lot of calories on the court, especially during intense competition. In fact, it is not unreasonable for players to expend 600-800 calories per hour during competitive recreational singles play. It is important for players to balance this caloric loss during play by consuming enough calories and ensuring the meals contain all of the essential nutrients.

Which nutrients provide the most support for such an expenditure of energy? Carbohydrates, fats, proteins, water, vitamins, and minerals all are important for the tennis player; however, carbohydrates and fats are the primary sources of energy for tennis. Fats are typically used for fuel during low to moderate intensity exercise. However, as the intensity of play increases during a match and energy expenditure goes up, the body's emphasis shifts to utilizing more carbohydrate and proportionately less fat for fuel. This is because the body can break down carbohydrates to supply energy for muscle contraction at a much faster rate than fat can be broken down and converted to usable energy.

The intermittent nature of tennis play reduces the "overall intensity" in a match. In other words, there is not a continuous high demand for energy within any specific muscle group and some recovery can occur between points. Consequently, even during intense singles, fat is used to supply considerable energy throughout the course of the match. During the latter part of a tennis match, protein could become a contributor in meeting a player's energy demands, especially if the pre-match and during-play dietary carbohydrate intake is inadequate. This, of course, is undesirable since it is typically muscle that is broken down to meet the increased energy needs of the body.

Players also need to consider that, as with any vigorous physical activity, playing tennis produces a considerable amount of body heat, which can cause a player's core body temperature to rise. Sweating is typically the most effective and most utilized on-court method for dissipating heat in either hot or cool weather. This poses a significant challenge to many tennis players since the water lost through sweat must be replaced to avoid dehydration and impaired performance. If the fluid lost via sweat is no properly balanced by fluid intake on the court, a tennis player may become dehydrated and overheated, and likely will experience 'premature' fatigue and possibly lose the match. More severely, heat exhaustion, heat cramps, or even worse, heat stroke may ultimately ensue.

Fueling Tennis Players

The number of calories that you need to play tennis depends on your age, gender, training intensity and duration, and competition schedule. Tennis is a highintensity sport involving hundreds of short bursts of activity. Most points in tennis last less than 10 seconds. But tennis is also an endurance sport. When you play long matches, there are only 25 seconds of rest between points and only 90 seconds between games. It is very important to have enough energy and fluids.

- You use 5 to 11 calories per minute when you play singles recreational tennis and 3.4 to 7.7 calories per minute when you play doubles. Competitive tennis players can burn 6.4 to 14.4 calories per minute of activity.
- You need to eat at least 2.7 grams of carbohydrate per pound of body weight per day (6 g/kg/day). When you are on the court several hours a day, you need to eat more carbohydrate: 3.2 to 4.5 grams per pound per day (7 to 10 g/kg/day).
- Eating carbohydrate can improve the quality of your stroke in the final stages of a long tennis match. Eat 100 grams of carbohydrate about 30 minutes before a match, and eat an additional 50 grams every 2 hours during the match.

— Good sources of carbohydrate include whole grain breads and cereals, fruits, and vegetables.

— Tennis players need 0.55 to 0.8 grams of protein per pound of body weight per day (1.2 to 1.7 g/kg/day). Eating more protein than this does not improve your tennis.

— Good sources of protein include fish, chicken, turkey, beef, low-fat milk, cheese, yogurt, eggs, nuts, and soy foods (tofu, soy nuts, and soy burgers).

— Carbohydrate is a better fuel than fat for playing tennis, but you do need to eat some fat every day to stay healthy. Also, your body will burn fat for energy during long matches. Eat at least 0.45 grams of fat per pound of body weight per day (1 g/kg). Choose heart-healthy fats, such as canola oil, olive oil, and nuts.

Fluid Needs

Tennis players need a planned schedule for drinking fluids. Drinking enough fluids improves performance and helps prevent heat illness during training and competition.

— Drink on a schedule. Drink 2 cups of water or sport drink 2 hours before practice or competition.

— On hot, humid days and when the sun is at its peak, choose sport drinks.

— During matches, keep a bottle of sport drink in a cooler on the bench and drink 5 to 10 ounces at every changeover. Most players can easily drink 5 ounces.

— After matches, drink enough to replace lost water weight.

— Drink 3 cups of fluid for every pound lost during practice or a match.

— Check the color of your urine. A pale, straw color means you are hydrated.

— If you get cramps, you may need more fluid and sodium.

— If you get cramps often, add ½ teaspoon of table salt to 32 ounces of sport drink, or choose an "endurance" formula sport drink. It will contain more sodium than a regular sport drink.

Commonly Used Supplements

Creatine supplementation may help athletes in highintensity, short-duration activities, like the short bursts of play in tennis.

Creatine may help you recover more quickly from workouts, which could help you train harder.

Creatine monohydrate powder is a common creatine supplement. The recommended dose is 3 to 5 grams per day spread throughout the day. Taking more than that amount does not increase the benefits.

Creatine does not help with endurance, and it may cause weight gain.

Creatine is not recommended for athletes younger than 18 years because it is not known whether it is safe for use in people in that age group.

Energy bars and gels can provide added calories to your food plan. Choose an energy bar that provides more carbohydrate than protein or fat.

Energy gels can give you extra calories and carbohydrates for day-long tournaments. Gels are concentrated carbohydrates, and you should drink extra fluids when you use them.

Improve Performance

1. Replace the fluids, electrolytes, and carbohydrates that your body loses in long matches. This will help you recover faster and get you ready for the next match. A sport drink can help replace fluid, electrolytes, and carbohydrates. Drink sport drinks at the end of the match to start to recover. At the meal after your match, eat plenty of carbohydrate-rich foods, salt your food, and drink plenty of fluids.
2. Train your body to tolerate fluids during exercise.

   Many tennis players don't drink enough because they feel like fluids "slosh" around in their stomachs. To get over this feeling, start by drinking a small amount (about ½ cup) at the change-over when you train, and gradually increase the amount you drink to 1 cup. Drinking more helps move fluids into your blood and muscles where they are needed.
3. Work with a sports dietitian to create a food and fluid plan. A sports dietitian can help you plan prematch, match, and postmatch foods and fluids that fit your training schedule and your lifestyle.

Ten Commandments of Tennis Nutrition and Fitness

— Thou shalt maintain a balanced diet.

— Thou shalt drink plenty of water and fluids.

— Thou shalt not consume high quantities of junk food.

— Thou shalt consume foods high in carbohydrates before matches and tournaments.

— Thou shalt eat two or three hours before competition.

— Thou shalt seek professional advice concerning weight, body composition, nutrition, and aerobic and strength training guidelines appropriate for your physical make-up.

— Thou shalt emphasize body composition rather than weight as a guide to a healthy body.

— Thou shalt stretch daily, and before and after matches.

— Thou shalt perform exercises to increase strength and flexibility that is specifically needed for tennis.

— Thou shalt regularly perform aerobic workouts to increase stamina and enjoy a long and healthy tennis life.

Common Nutrition Issues

The training and playing schedules of many elite players set up large energy and carbohydrate requirements. At a lower level of play, carbohydrate needs may not be as great, but may still be beyond the level supplied by the typical Australian diet. Active tennis players need to make nutrient-dense carbohydrate foods such as pasta, rice, bread, cereal, vegetables, fruit and sweetened dairy products the focus of meals and snacks. Players in heavy training need to start recovery nutrition tactics immediately after each training session. Ideally, players should aim to have 50-100 grams of carbohydrate within 30 minutes of finishing training. Recovery snacks should be combined with fluid to replace any fluid lost during the session.

Body-Fat Levels

Many players, especially females, do not automatically arrive at the body-fat level that does them justice on the court. Being overweight will reduce speed and stamina, and increase suffering during hot days on the court. The first step to reducing body fat is to forget methods claiming to be magic or miraculous and adopt a consistent, long-term approach to body fat maintenance. **Try the following:**

- Consult a dietitian to decide exactly how much you need to eat, as distinct from what you would like to eat.
- Avoid letting yourself get too hungry. A small but well-timed snack will prevent you from over-eating later on.
- Eat slowly so you enjoy your food and can recognise when you have eaten enough.
- Enjoy high fire foods as they are more filling.
- Drink water before and during your meal.
- Take care with high-energy fluids such as juice, cordial and soft drink. It is easy to quaff litres of kilojoules.
- Include your favourite foods but in small quantities.
- Target fat, alcohol and sugar.
- Keep a food record to help identify why you eat - are you hungry or just bored, upset, depressed, tired etc?
- Find non-food ways of rewarding yourself.

Fluid Intake During Matches and Training

Tennis is often played in sweltering conditions. Court surface temperatures of 500C have been reported from centre court during the Australian Open. When matches drag out to three hours or more players can amass large sweat losses. Fluid losses can also be quite large during training sessions. However, fluid intake can be less as players are not prompted to drink by change of ends as they are during matches. The following sweat loss and fluid intake data has been reported for Division I American University tennis players during singles matches.

Tips for better drinking during tennis are:

— Follow a plan of fluid intake before, during and after matches to keep reasonable pace with sweat losses.
— Use pre-and post-weighing activities to monitor fluid losses over training and try to keep these under 1kg.
— Be aware of your sweat losses during a match, and be especially aggressive on hot and humid days.
— Keep a supply of cool and refreshing fluids courtside and grab a drink as appropriate. On some days it may be sufficient to drink between sets, but it is probably good practice to grab a quick drink as you change ends after every second game.
— While water is adequate to replace fluid losses, there are additional advantages in using a carbohydrate-electrolyte beverage such as a sports drink during long, intense matches.
— After the match, replace any remaining fluid deficit to prevent problems of chronic dehydration throughout the tournament.

Tournament Tennis

Tournament tennis is challenging from many nutritional viewpoints. Apart from the considerations of being away from home - even for a weekend tournament - the tournament schedule places great demands on nutritional strategies for recovery, and on a player's flexibility and ingenuity. Not only must a player be committed to looking after fluid and carbohydrate needs between matches, but they must do so without a definite timetable of their day's activities.

Since each day's match draw is determined by the results of the previous day's play, players receive short notice about their daily schedule. Forward planning is also made difficult by the loose nature of the daily timetable. While the starting time for the first match of each session can be set, all other matches simply follow in succession. Given the great range of duration of matches, it is often difficult for a player to predict accurately the time of their matches. Tournament players must learn to be adaptable with their eating plans - having a clear idea of the goals of competition nutrition, but being prepared to handle all possible outcomes in a day's play.

Life on the Circuit

Elite tennis players can look forward to a life of travelling - around Australia and around the world. While this can be exciting, it can also be stressful. It is often hard to meet nutritional needs in unfamiliar surroundings, especially when time and finances are limited. Unusual foods, different standards of food hygiene, limited food availability and interference with usual routines can see athletes either gaining weight or failing to meet their nutritional requirements. The following tips may help:

— Be clear about your nutritional goals and stay committed while travelling.

— Do some investigation to find out what to expect at your destination.

— Plan your accommodation with meals in mind. Organising an apartment with cooking facilities gives you more control over your meals and can keep food costs down. If you choose not to cook, make sure your accommodation is conveniently located near shops and restaurants.

— Take a supply of snacks with you so you always have access to something suitable. Cereal bars, low-fat 2-minute noodles, sports drinks, breakfast cereal and rice cakes are good options to pack.

— Make good choices in restaurants. Beware of hidden fat in restaurant meals.

9

Table Tennis

Table tennis is a sport in which two or four players hit a lightweight ball back and forth to each other with bats (also sometimes called racquets or paddles). The game takes place on a table divided by a net. Players must allow a ball played towards them only one bounce on their side of the table and must return it so that it bounces on the opponent's side. If the ball doesn't land on the opponent's side then it's a dead ball unless the other opponent hits the ball with their bat. Play is fast and demands quick reactions. A skilled player can impart spin to the ball, which makes its bounce and its reaction on the opponent's bat difficult to predict or return with confidence.

Table tennis is very popular, especially in East Asia and is among the most popular sports in the world in terms of player numbers, as well as one of the newest of the major sports.

Table tennis is a game where two or four players hit a ball with paddles back and forth to each other on a table, in a manner similar to tennis. The rules are slightly different, but the concept is quite similar. In singles play, the ball is not required to cross from the server's right-hand court to the receiver's right-hand court (or left to left) as it is in tennis. However, serving across is required in doubles play. Ball spin, speed, placement, strategy and tactics play an important part in competitive table tennis matches. The speed of the ball can vary from slow serves with much spin to smashes that travel as fast as 112.5 kilometers per hour (69.9 miles per hour).

The game is played on a 274 cm (9 ft.) × 152.5 cm (5 ft.) × 76 cm (2.5 ft.) high playing surface. The International Table Tennis Federation requires an area not less than 14 m (46 ft) long, 7 m (23 ft) wide and 5 m (16 ft) high for competitions. No limitations in size or shape are specified. Modern paddles usually have a thin layer of rubber covering the paddle's striking surface. The rubber may have pimples pointing outwards or inwards, as well as a thin layer of sponge between the plywood center and the rubber surface.

Since spin plays a large role in the modern sport of table tennis, the composition of the rubber and the combination of sponge and rubber is designed to maximize the amount of spin and speed a player can impart onto the ball. Other technological improvements include the use of carbon or other synthetic layers as part of the blade to increase the size of the sweet spot or the stiffness of the blade.

The ball used in table tennis has a diameter of 40 mm, is made of celluloid, and is completely hollow. A three star rating on a ball usually implies a top quality ball, in relation to its bounce, roundness and their respective consistency between balls of the same make and type.

The winner is the first to score 11 points, with each player alternating serves every two points. At 10-10 (or deuce) the players alternate with every serve; the winner is then the first person to gain a clear two points advantage over his opponent. The 11 point game is an International Table Tennis Federation (ITTF) change which occurred in 2001. All games played at national level and at international tournaments (ITTF) are played to 11 points in either a best of five (5) games (preliminaries) or best of seven (7) games format (championship matches).

History

The game has its origins in England as an after-dinner amusement for upper-class Victorians in the 1880s. Mimicking the game of tennis in an indoor environment, everyday objects were originally enlisted to act as the equipment. A line of books would be the net, a rounded top of a Champagne cork or knot of string as the ball, and a cigar box lid as the bat. The popularity of the game led game manufacturers to sell the equipment commercially. Early bats were often pieces of parchment stretched upon a frame, and the sound generated in play gave the game its first nicknames of *"whiff-whaff"* and *"Ping-pong."*

A number of sources indicate that the game was first brought to the attention of Hamley's of Regent Street under the name "Gossima". The name "ping-pong" was in wide use before English manufacturer J. Jaques & Son Ltd trademarked it in 1901. The name "Ping-Pong" then came to be used for the game played by the rather expensive Jaques equipment, with other manufacturers calling theirs table tennis. A similar situation came to exist in the United States where Jaques sold the rights to the "Ping-Pong" name to Parker Brothers.

The next major innovation was by James Gibb, an English enthusiast of the game, who discovered novelty celluloid balls on a trip to the U.S. in 1901 and found them to be the ideal balls for the game. This was followed by E.C. Goode who in 1903 invented the modern version of the bat by fixing a sheet of pimpled, or stippled, rubber to the wooden blade. Table tennis was growing in popularity by 1901 when table tennis tournaments were being organized, books on table tennis were being written, and an unofficial world championship was held in 1902.

During the early 20th century the game was banned in Russia due to the belief that was held by the rulers at the time that playing the game had an adverse effect on players' eyesight. In 1921, the Table Tennis Association was founded in England, and the International Table Tennis Federation followed in 1926. London hosted the first official world championship in 1927. Table tennis was introduced as an Olympic sport at the Olympics in 1988. In the 1950s bats that used a rubber sheet combined with a underlaying sponge layer changed the game dramatically, introducing greater spin and speed. These were introduced to England by the sports goods manufacturers S.W. Hancock Ltd. and the Hancock bat gave Johnny Leach the edge when he became World Champion in 1949. The use of speed glue increased the spin and speed even further, resulting in changes to the equipment to "slow the game down."

Toward the end of 2000, the ITTF instituted several rules changes aimed at making table tennis more viable as a televised spectator sport. First, the older 38 mm balls were officially replaced by 40 mm balls. This increased the ball's air resistance and effectively slowed down the game. By that time, players had begun increasing the thickness of the fast sponge layer on their bats, which made the game excessively fast, and difficult to watch on television.

Secondly, the ITTF changed from a 21 to an 11 point scoring system. This was intended to make games more fast-paced and exciting. The ITTF also changed the rules on service to prevent a player from hiding the ball during service, in order to increase the average length of rallies and to reduce the server's advantage. Variants of the sport have emerged. "Large-ball" table tennis uses a 44 mm ball which slows down the game significantly. This has seen some acceptance by players who have a hard time with the extreme spins and speeds of the 40 mm game. The ball weighs 2.47 grams.

There is a move towards reviving the table tennis game that existed prior to the introduction of sponge rubber. Classic table tennis or "Hardbat" table tennis players reject the speed and spin of reversed sponge rubber, preferring the 1940-60s style of no-sponge, short pimpled rubber of play which makes defense less difficult by decreasing the speed and eliminating any meaningful magnus effect of spin. Because hardbat killer shots are almost impossible to hit against a skilled player, hardbat matches focus on the strategic side of table tennis, requiring skillful maneuvering of the opponent before an attack can be successful.

Equipment

The ball

The international rules specify that the game is played with a light 2.7 gram, 40 mm (formerly 38 mm) diameter ball. The ball is required to have a coefficient of restitution of 0.94. The 40 mm ball was introduced at the 2003 World Table Tennis Championship. However, this created some controversy as the Chinese National Team argued that this was merely to give non-Chinese players a better chance of winning. A 40 mm table tennis ball is slower and less "spinny" than a 38 mm one. The ball is made of a high-bouncing gas-filled celluloid ball, colored white or orange, with a matte finish. The choice of ball color is made according to the table color and its surroundings. For example, a white ball is easier to see on a green or blue table than it is on a grey table. A star on the ball indicates the quality of the ball. 3 stars is the highest indicating that it is of the highest quality.

The table

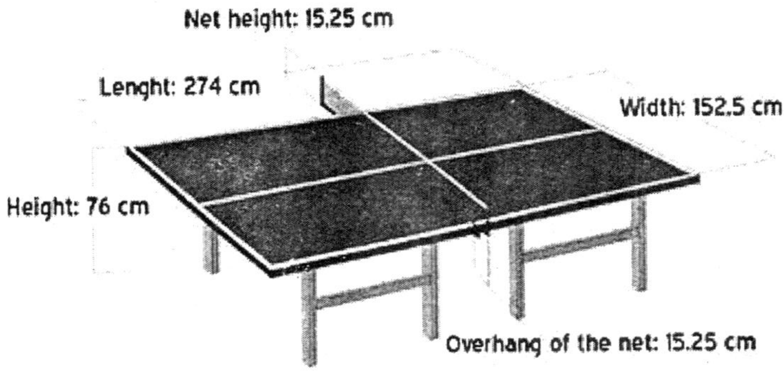

Table is 2.74 m (9 ft) long, 1.525 m (5 feet) wide, and 76 cm (30 inches) high with a masonite or similarly manufactured timber, layered with a smooth, low-friction coating. The table or playing surface is divided into two halves by a 15.25 cm (6 inch) high net.

The bat

Players are equipped with a bat composed of a wooden blade covered with rubber on one or two sides depending on the grip of the player.

Table tennis regulations allow different surfaces on each side of the bat. The different types of surfaces provide various levels of spin or speed, or in some cases, nullifies spin. For example, a player may have a rubber that provides much spin on one side of his bat, and no spin on the other side of the bat. By flipping the bat in play, different types of returns are possible. To help a player distinguish between different types of rubber used by his opposing player, international rules specify that one side must be red while the other side must be black. The player has the right to inspect his opponent's bat before a match to see the type of rubber used and what color it is. Despite high speed play and rapid exchanges, a player can see clearly what side of the bat was used to hit the ball.

Recent years have seen an advancement in technology of table tennis blades. Materials of different properties may be combined with the wood in the blade to enhance its playing performance. Many blades today feature one or more carbon layers within them to enhance their 'sweet spot', and to give the player a greater margin of error when playing powerful shots. Materials incorporated into table tennis blades today include titanium, acrylate, aramids, and aluminium.

The rubber coating may be of pimpled rubber, with the pimples outward, or it may be a rubber that is composed of two materials, a sponge layer, covered by a pimpled rubber, with the pimples pointed inwards or outwards. Some bats are not covered with rubber at all, because a "naked" bat is believed to be more resistant to a spin. However, it is illegal to use these types of bats in competition as they are not approved by the ITTF. Some types of rubbers are also not approved. Approved rubbers have the ITTF emblem on the base of the rubber.

Players have many choices and variations in rubber sheets on their bat. Although bats may be purchased with rubber by the manufacturer, most serious tournament players will create a customized bat. A player selects a blank blade (i.e. a bat without rubber), based on his playing style. The type of wood and synthetic layers used to make up the blade will provide a slower or faster blade. The player can choose from different types of rubber sheets which will provide a certain level of spin, speed and specific playing characteristics.

Normally, a sheet of rubber is glued to a blade using rubber cement and not removed until the rubber wears out or becomes damaged. In the 1980s, a new technique was developed where the player would use a special glue called speed glue to apply the rubber every time he played. The glue would help provide more spin and speed by providing a "catapult" effect. This technique is known as "regluing" and has become a standard technique for top players.

The surface of a bat will develop a smooth glossy patina with use. The blade surface needs to be regularly cleaned to ensure it retains a high friction surface to impart spin to the ball. Players use a commercial cleaner, or just water and detergent as cleaning agents.

Bat construction and new rubber technology (skilled elite players typically select and attach the rubber to their own bats and glue them before every match) contribute significantly to the amount of deviation from the expected ball flight path. The fairly recent development of speed glue speeds up the departure of the ball from the rubber considerably, though at the cost of some ball control.

Different types of rubber sheets

— *Inverted (non-Chinese):* This is the most widely used rubber type. The surface is smooth, with the pimpled side facing inwards toward the blade. This enables the player to generate high levels of spin and speed. Spin is mainly generated not by the action of the topsheet alone, but also by the ball sinking into the sponge and allowing greater surface area to contact the ball.

— *Inverted (Chinese):* Chinese rubbers typically have stickier (or "tackier") topsheets. Spin is generated mainly by the topsheet, as opposed to the sponge, which is relatively more condensed and firmer. The result is usually a far better short game and potential power capabilities than normal inverted.

— *Short pimples (or "pips"):* Short pimples-out rubbers are usually used by close-to-the-table hitters (for example, Liu Guoliang). They do not generate as much spin as inverted rubbers, but also make the user less susceptible to the opponent's spin. Speed generated from a short pip rubber is generally faster than the inverted with the same sponge. Depending on the thickness of the sponge it is also possible to play a chopping game with short pimples by varying the spin of the return. Whilst blocking and attacking a "dead ball" effect is often noticed. Ding Song is an exponent of this style.

— *Long pimples (or "pips"):* Long pimples-out rubbers carry relatively long and soft pips. They do not have the ability to generate any real spin of their own, but feed off the opponent's spin, to allow the user to confuse the opponent and upset their rhythm. Long pips are not very susceptible to the opponent's incoming spin, and tends to "return" the opponent's spin back upon impact, as the pips bend and slide. They are usually used by close-to-the-table blockers, or choppers. They are usually only used on the backhand side, as they offer very limited attacking capabilities. Depending on the grip of the sides of the pimples and the thickness of the sponge it is also possible to play an aggressive game with long pips, though with not much spin capability.

— *Anti-spin*: Anti-spin rubbers may look similar to inverted ones, but the surface is really slick. Like long pimples, they cannot generate much real spin, but just allows the user to produce a no-spin ball. Anti-spin is also not very susceptible to the opponents incoming spin, due to the low coefficient of friction of the rubber's surface. This is also used to confuse the opponent, and is not widely used at international level.

Game Play

Starting a game

In top-flight competition, service is decided by a coin toss. At lower levels it is common for one player (or the umpire/scorer) to hide the ball in one or the other hand (usually hidden under the table), allowing the other player to guess which hand the ball is in. The correct or incorrect guess gives the "winner" the option to choose to serve, or to choose which side of the table to use. In recreational games, the players may have a rally for a minimum set number of 10 hits, after which the rally is played out, with the winner either choosing to serve or choosing the table side. Others use the "P-O-N-G" or "P-I-N-G" method rallying back and forth spelling a letter of P-O-N-G or P-I-N-G after every hit. After P-O-N-G or P-I-N-G is spelled the person to win the rally also wins the serve.

Service

In game play, the player serving the ball commences a point. Standing behind the end of the table, with the ball in the palm of one hand - over the table's height - and the bat in the other, the server tosses the ball without spin, upward, at least sixteen centimeters (approximately 6 inches).

He or she then must hit the ball such that it bounces once on his or her half of the table, and then bounces at least one time on the opponent's half. If the ball strikes the net but does not strike the opponent's half of the table, then a point is awarded to the opponent. However, if the ball hits the net, but nevertheless goes over and bounces on the other side, it is called a let (or net-in). Play stops, and the ball must be served again with no penalty. Unlike the old service rules, where a player may only commit three lets, now a player may commit any number of lets without penalty.

If the service is "good", then the opponent must then make a "good" return — by returning the ball before it bounces on his or her side of the table a second time. Returning the serve is one of the most difficult parts of the game, as the server's first move is often the least predictable.

Hitting the Ball

Any hitting of the ball must be done such that the ball passes over or around the net. If the ball is struck such that it travels around the net, but still lands on the opponent's side of the table, the hit is legal and play should be continued. If the opponent cannot return it over (or around) the net and make it bounce on your side, then you win the point.

Scoring

Points are awarded to the opponent for any of several errors in play:

— Allowing the ball to bounce on one's own side twice

— Not hitting the ball after it has bounced on one's own side

— Having the ball bounce on one's own side after hitting it

— Hitting the ball before it has bounced on one's own side of the table

— Double hitting the ball. Note that the hand below the wrist is considered part of the bat and making a good return off one's hand or fingers is allowed, but hitting one's hand or fingers and subsequently hitting the bat is a double strike and an error.
— Allowing the ball to strike anything other than the bat (see above for definition of the bat)
— Causing the ball not to bounce on the opponent's half (i.e., not making a "good" return)
— Placing one's free hand on the playing surface or moving the playing surface
— Offering and failing to make a good serve (i.e., making a service toss and failing to strike the ball fairly into play)
— Making an illegal serve: (e.g., one preceded by a player's hiding the ball or his failing to toss the ball at least 16 centimeters (six inches) in the air).
— Hitting the net with bat or any body part, or moving the table.

Alternation of service

Service alternates between opponents every two points (regardless of winner of the rally) until a player reaches 11 points with at least a two-point lead, or until both players have 10 points a piece. If both players reach 10 points, then service alternates after each point, until one player gains a two-point advantage.

In doubles, service alternates every two points between sides, but also rotates between players on the same team. At the end of every two points, the receiving player becomes the server, and the partner of the serving player becomes the receiver.

In the older 21-point game system, service would alternate every 5 points. If both players reached a score of

20, then service would alternate each point until one player gains a two-point advantage. When a match point occurs the server is allowed three attempts at serving and 2 lets before he loses the point.

Series of games

After each game, players switch sides of the table and in the fifth or seventh, game "for the match", players switch sides when the first player scores 5 points, regardless of whose turn it is to serve. In competition play, matches are typically best of five or seven games.

Recreational variations

Some recreational players may choose to use a volleyball style system of scoring and play. Such variations include, but are not limited to, allowing the let serve, not requiring the server to hit the ball on his half of the table first (but still allowing it), allowing the volleying of returns, and relaxing other small rules in doubles to make the game easier to play. Common recreational scoring styles include best-of-three-game side out scoring to 15, 21, 25, or 30 points per game with a third game being played rally style to 15; best-of-five-game rally style play with each game, save the fifth (to 15), played to 30 points; and traditional tennis scoring.

Doubles game

In addition to games between individual players, pairs may also play table tennis. In doubles, all the rules of single play apply except for the following. A line painted along the long axis of the table to create doubles courts bisects the table. This line's only purpose is to facilitate the doubles service rule, which is that service, must originate from the right hand "box" in such a way that the first bounce of the serve bounces once in said right hand box and then must bounce at least once in the opponent side's right hand box (far left box for server).

Play then continues normally with the exception that players must alternate hitting the ball. For example, after a player serves the receiving player make his or her return, the server's partner returns the ball and then the service receiver's partner would play the ball. In wheelchair doubles side. The point proceeds this way until one side fails to make a legal return and the point is then awarded to the other team. Also, when the game reaches the final set, the teams must switch side and the team that receives the service must switch receiver when one of the teams reach 5 points. Singles and doubles are both played in international competition, including the Olympic Games since 1988 and the Commonwealth Games since 2002. In 2005, the ITTF has announced that doubles table tennis will only be featured as a part of teams events in the 2008 Olympics.

Styles of play

Grip

Competitive table tennis players grip their bats in a variety of ways. The manner in which competitive players grip their bats can be classified into two major families of styles. One is described as *penhold,* and the other *shakehand*. The Laws of Table Tennis do not prescribe the manner in which one must grip the bat, and numerous variations on gripping styles exist.

Penhold

The penhold grip is so-named because one grips the bat similarly to the way one holds a writing instrument. The style of play among penhold players can vary greatly from player to player. The style, usually referred to as the Chinese penhold style, involves curling the middle, ring, and fourth finger back. In contrast, another style, sometimes referred to as the Japanese penhold, involves splaying those three fingers out across the back of the bat.

Penhold styles are popular among players originating from Asian nations such as China, Taiwan, Japan, and South Korea. Traditionally, penhold players use only one side of the bat to hit the ball during normal play. The side which is in contact with the last three fingers is generally not used. However, the Chinese have developed a new technique in which a penholder utilizes both sides of the bat. This is referred to as the *reverse penhold backhand* (RPB).

Shakehand

The shakehand grip is so-named because one grips the bat similarly to the way one performs a handshake. The grip is sometimes colloquially referred to as a "tennis grip" or a "Western grip." The shakehand grip is most popular among players originating in Western nations. Today, though, there are many Asian players using the shakehand grip.

Unusual grips

V-grip

An experimental style being developed in China, it is held by forming a "V for victory" sign and gripping the blade between the forefinger and middle finger, whilst having the other fingers rest under and on top of the handle; it requires a modified blade to grip successfully. A noticeable spin benefit is noticed due to the longer lever and mechanics utilized in the forehand and backhand (much like those found in the Western grip in tennis).

Seemiller grip

A grip that was made famous by Danny Seemiller, an American champion. This grip is a variation of the shakehand grip. In this grip, the forefinger and thumb are placed on the same side of the bat, which allows the backhand and forehand shots to use the same side of the rubber. This grip also has the nickname "windshield wiper" due to the motion of the backhand and forehand.

Types of Shots

In table tennis, the strokes break down into generally offensive (producing topspin) and defensive (producing backspin). Spin exceptions are the smash, block, and lob. The types of strokes include backhand and forehand.

Offensive Strokes

Speed drive

In table tennis it is not similar to strokes from racket sports like tennis. The bat is primarily *perpendicular* to the direction of the stroke, and most of the energy applied to the ball results in *speed* rather than *spin*, creating a shot that does not arc much, but is fast enough that it can be difficult to return. A speed drive is used mostly for keeping the ball in play, applying pressure on the opponent and potentially opening up an opportunity for a more powerful attack.

Loop drive

It is essentially the reverse of the speed drive. The bat is much more *parallel* to the direction of the stroke ("closed") and the bat thus *grazes* the ball, resulting in a large amount of topspin. A good loop drive will arc quite a bit, and once striking the opponent's side of the table will jump forward, much like a kick serve in tennis. A loop drive is dangerous because of its topspin — while not as difficult to return as a speed drive, it is more likely to rebound off the opponent's bat at a very high angle, setting up an easy smash on the follow up. As the loop drive requires a lot of topspin, players generally use their entire body to generate the movement required. Variations in spin and speed adds to effectiveness of this shot.

Chinese players categorized loop-drives in 3 variations based on trajectories:

1. The "Loop"

Produces a more pronounced loopy arc, with a higher trajectory and extreme topspin, but is typically slower.

2. The "Rush"

Produces a flatter trajectory than a typical "Loop" but carries much stronger topspin than a regular speed-drive. It can be as fast as a speed-drive, and in modern table tennis has come to replace it in virtually all cases. The ball seems to "rush" forward and downward upon hitting the table, and hence the nickname. (Compared to the "kicking" or "jumping" actions resulted from the high-arc "Loop")

3. The "Hook"

Similar to a regular Loop, but carries a tilted topspin (or is referred as the "top-side" spin), it bounces sideways and downward upon hitting the table. Similar but stronger than the defensive "side-drive" described below.

Counter drive

Usually a counter attack against drives (normally high loop drives). You have to close the bat and stay close to the ball (try to predict its path). The bat is held closed and near to the ball, which is hit with a short movement "off the bounce" (before reaching the highest point) so that the ball travels faster to the other side. If performed correctly, a well-timed, accurate counter-drive can be as effective as a smash.

Flip (or Flick in Europe)

When a player tries to attack a ball that has not bounced beyond the edge of the table, he/she does not have the room to wind up in a *backswing*. The ball *may still be attacked*, however, and the resulting shot is called flip because the backswing is compressed into a quick wrist action. A flip is not a single stroke and can resemble either a drive or a loop in its characteristics. What identifies the stroke is instead whether the backswing is compressed into a short wrist flick. Also known as *?? "harai"* in Japanese.

Smash

The offensive trump card in table tennis. A player will typically execute a smash when his or her opponent has returned a ball that bounces too high and/or too close to the net. *Smashing* is essentially self-explanatory — large backswing and rapid acceleration imparting as much speed on the ball as possible. The goal of a smash is to get the ball to move so quickly that the opponent simply cannot return it. Because the ball speed is the main aim of this shot, often the spin on the ball is something other than topspin. Sidespin can be used effectively with a smash to alter the ball's trajectory significantly, although most intermediate players will smash the ball with little or no spin.

An offensive table-tennis player will think of a rally as a build-up to a winning smash; only a calculated series of smashes can guarantee a point against a good opponent. However, most players will be able to return at most one or two smashes consistently. Provided that the opponent is not too close to the table or too far away from the ball, a smash can be lobbed, chopped, blocked or even counter-looped, albeit with some difficulty. A player who smashes generally works out a series of smashes (and possibly drop-shots) to rush the opponent out of position, put him off balance, or both. Smashers who fail to do this find it difficult to win a point against an excellent defense.

Defensive strokes

Slice

The *slice* or is analogous to the *speed drive* in some respects — it is very simple, usually used for keeping the point alive and creating offensive opportunities. A *slice* resembles a tennis slice: the bat cuts underneath the ball, imparting backspin and causing the ball to float slowly to the other side of the table. While not obvious, a slice can be difficult to attack because the *backspin* on the ball causes it to drop toward the table upon striking the opponent's bat – in order to attack a *slice,* a player must *lift* the ball back over the net. Often, the best option is to simply *slice* the ball back again, which repeats and results in *slicing rallies*. Otherwise, another option is to *flip* or *drive* the ball, only when it is far enough away from the net.

Slicing can have its advantages, but it's a shot worth avoiding. Players should only slice when their opponent makes easy mistakes. Offensive players should only slice for variation and not for general rallies. A slice can easily be counter-looped into the opposite corner, if it doesn't drop short enough on the table. The goal of most player's *slice* is to make it too short to be attacked upon, rather than attempting to over-spin the opponent.

Chop

A *chop* or *cut* is the defensive, backspin counterpart to the offensive *loop drive.* A *chop* is essentially a bigger, heavier *slice,* taken well back from the table. The bat face points primarily horizontally, perhaps a little bit upward, and the direction of the stroke is *straight down.* The object of a defensive *chop* is to *match* the topspin of the opponent's shot with your own bat speed. A good *chop* will float nearly horizontally back to the table, in some cases having so much backspin that the ball actually *rises.*

A *chop* such as this can be *extremely* difficult to return due to the enormous amount of backspin. Sometimes a defensive player can impart no spin on the ball during a *chop,* or frequently add right- or left-hand spin to the ball. This may further confuse his/her opponent. *Chops* are difficult to execute, but are devastating when completed properly because it takes a tremendous amount of *topspin* on a *loop drive* to return the ball back over the net.

Block

The *block* or *short* is a simple shot, barely worthy of being called a "stroke," but nonetheless can be *devastating* against an attacking opponent. A *block* is executed by simply putting the bat in front of the ball — the ball rebounds back toward the opponent with nearly as much energy as it came in with. This is not as easy as it sounds, because the ball's spin, speed, and location all influence the correct angle of a *block.*

Disregarding the difficulty of a block, it is very possible for an opponent to execute a perfect *loop, drive,* or *smash,* only to have the *blocked* shot come back at him just as fast. Due to the powei involved in offensive strokes, often an opponent simply cannot recover quickly enough, and will be unable to return his own shot *blocked* back to him/her. *Blocks* almost always produce the same spin as was received, which is nearly always topspin.

Push-Block

High level players may use what is called *push block* or *active block,* adding speed to the ball (with a small topspin movement). When playing in the *Penhold Grip,* many players use *push blocks* when being pressured on the backhand. Chinese pen-hold players refer it as *push-block* as they literally "push" their backhand forward, instead of simply blocking it.

Side Drive

This spin is alternately used as a defensive and offensive maneuver. The premise of this move is to put a spin on the ball either to the *right* or the *left* of the bat. The execution of this move is similar to a slice, but to the right or left instead of down. This spin will result in the ball curving to the side but bouncing in the opposite direction when the opponent returns it. Do not attempt a right-side spin (moving your arm to the right when hitting the ball) when too close to the left side of the table, and visa versa. To return, simply execute the same sided spin as your opponent just gave you.

Lob

The defensive *lob* is possibly the most visually-impressive shot in the sport of table tennis, and it is deceptive in its simplicity. To execute a *lob,* a defensive player first backs off the table 8-10 feet (2.5 to 3 m, advanced players sometimes go 20 feet or 6 m or more); then, the stroke itself consists of simply lifting the ball to an enormous height before it falls back to the opponent's side of the table. A *lob* is inherently a creative shot, and can have nearly any kind of spin you can imagine.

Talented players use this fact to their advantage in order to control the point. For instance, though the opponent may *smash* the ball hard and fast, a good defensive *lob* could quite possibly be even *harder* to return due to the unpredictability (and heavy amounts) of the spin on the ball. Thus, though backed off the table by tens of feet and apparently running and leaping just to *reach* the ball, a good defensive player can still *win* the point using good *lobs*.

Stop

Stop (or *drop shot*) is a high level stroke, used as another variation for close-to-table strokes (like *harai* and *slice*). You have to position the body close to the ball and just let the ball touch the bat (without any hand movement) in a way that the ball stays close to the net with almost no speed and spin and touches the other side of the table more than twice if the opponent doesn't reach it. This stroke should be used when opponents are far from the table and not prepared to get close to the table. This technique is most usually done by pen-holders and players who use long or short pimples. A very deceiving technique, this could result in the opponent failing to reach the ball after misjudging the *distance* of the ball. A perfectly executed stroke after a *topspin sequence* can win a point.

Competition

Competitive table tennis is popular in Asia and Europe and has been gaining attention in the United States. The most important international competitions are World Cup, World Championship, the Olympics and the ITTF Pro Tour, as well as continental competitions like European Championship, Euro Top-12, Asian Championship and Asian Games. China continues to dominate most world titles, while other strong teams come from East Asia and Europe including France, Germany, former Yugoslavia, Hong Kong, Japan, Korea, Singapore, Sweden, and Taiwan.

Besides, there are also professional competitions at the clubs level. The national league of countries like China, Germany, France, Belgium and Austria are some of the examples being at the highest level. There are also some important international club teams competitions such as the European Champions League and its former competition, the European Champions Cup, which the top club teams from different European countries compete.

There are also competitions in table tennis variants: "Hardbat", in which all competitors use a bat with small pips-out rubber (sponge is not allowed); and "Large ball", where a 44 mm ball is used to decrease the speed.

1. The Laws of Table Tennis

1.1 The Table

1.1.1 The upper surface of the table, known as the playing surface, shall be rectangular, 2.74m long and 1.525m wide, and shall lie in a horizontal plane 76cm above the floor.

1.1.2 The playing surface shall not include the vertical sides of the tabletop.

1.1.3 The playing surface may be of any material and shall yield a uniform bounce of about 23cm when a standard ball is dropped on to it from a height of 30cm.

1.1.4 The playing surface shall be uniformly dark coloured and matt, but with a white side line, 2cm wide, along each 2.74m edge and a white end line, 2cm wide, along each 1.525m edge.

1.1.5 The playing surface shall be divided into 2 equal courts by a vertical net running parallel with the end lines, and shall be continuous over the whole area of each court.

1.1.6 For doubles, each court shall be divided into 2 equal half-courts by a white centre line, 3mm wide, running parallel with the side lines; the centre line shall be regarded as part of each right half-court.

1.2 The Net Assembly

1.2.1 The net assembly shall consist of the net, its suspension and the supporting posts, including the clamps attaching them to the table.

1.2.2 The net shall be suspended by a cord attached at each end to an upright post 15.25cm high, the outside limits of the post being 15.25cm outside the side line.

1.2.3 The top of the net, along its whole length, shall be 15.25cm above the playing surface.

1.2.4 The bottom of the net, along its whole length, shall be as close as possible to the playing surface and the ends of the net shall be as close as possible to the supporting posts.

1.3 The Ball

1.3.1 The ball shall be spherical, with a diameter of 40mm.

1.3.2 The ball shall weigh 2.7g.

1.3.3 The ball shall be made of celluloid or similar plastics material and shall be white or orange, and matt.

1.4 The Racket

1.4.1 The racket may be of any size, shape or weight but the blade shall be flat and rigid.

1.4.2 At least 85% of the blade by thickness shall be of natural wood; an adhesive layer within the blade may be reinforced with fibrous material such as carbon fibre, glass fibre or compressed paper, but shall not be thicker than 7.5% of the total thickness or 0.35mm, whichever is the smaller.

1.4.3 A side of the blade used for striking the ball shall be covered with either ordinary pimpled rubber, with pimples outwards having a total thickness including adhesive of not more than 2mm, or sandwich rubber, with pimples inwards or outwards, having a total thickness including adhesive of not more than 4mm.

1.4.3.1 Ordinary pimpled rubber is a single layer of non-cellular rubber, natural or synthetic, with pimples evenly distributed over its surface at a density of not less than 10 per sq. cm and not more than 30 per sq. cm.

1.4.3.2 Sandwich rubber is a single layer of cellular rubber covered with a single outer layer of ordinary pimpled rubber, the thickness of the pimpled rubber not being more than 2mm.

1.4.4 The covering material shall extend up to but not beyond the limits of the blade, except that the part nearest the handle and gripped by the fingers may be left uncovered or covered with any material.

1.4.5 The blade, any layer within the blade and any layer of covering material or adhesive on a side used for striking the ball shall be continuous and of even thickness.

1.4.6 The surface of the covering material on a side of the blade, or of a side of the blade if it is left uncovered, shall be matt, bright red on one side and black on the other.

1.4.7 Slight deviations from continuity of surface or uniformity of colour due to accidental damage or wear may be allowed provided that they do not significantly change the characteristics of the surface.

1.4.8 At the start of a match and whenever he changes his racket during a match a player shall show his opponent and the umpire the racket he is about to use and shall allow them to examine it.

1.5 Definitions

1.5.1 A rally is the period during which the ball is in play.

1.5.2 The ball is in play from the last moment at which it is stationary on the palm of the free hand before being intentionally projected in service until the rally is decided as a let or a point.

1.5.3 A let is a rally of which the result is not scored.

1.5.4 A point is a rally of which the result is scored.

1.5.5 The racket hand is the hand carrying the racket.

1.5.6 The free hand is the hand not carrying the racket.

1.5.7 A player strikes the ball if he touches it in play with his racket, held in the hand, or with his racket hand below the wrist.

1.5.8 A player obstructs the ball if he, or anything he wears or carries, touches it in play when it is above or travelling towards the playing surface and has not passed beyond his end line, not having touched his court since last being struck by his opponent.

1.5.9 The server is the player due to strike the ball first in a rally.

1.5.10 The receiver is the player due to strike the ball second in a rally.

1.5.11 The umpire is the person appointed to control a match.

1.5.12 The assistant umpire is the person appointed to assist the umpire with certain decisions.

1.5.13 Anything that a player wears or carries includes anything that he was wearing or carrying, other than the ball, at the start of the rally.

1.5.14 The ball shall be regarded as passing over or around the net assembly if it passes anywhere other than between the net and the net post or between the net and the playing surface.

1.5.15 The end line shall be regarded as extending indefinitely in both directions.

1.6. A Good Service

1.6.1 Service shall start with the ball resting freely on the open palm of the server's stationary free hand.

1.6.2 The server shall then project the ball near vertically upwards, without imparting spin, so that it rises at least 16cm after leaving the palm of the free hand and then falls without touching anything before being struck.

1.6.3 As the ball is falling the server shall strike it so that it touches first his court and then, after passing over or around the net assembly, touches directly the receiver's court; in doubles, the ball shall touch successively the right half court of server and receiver.

1.6.4 From the start of service until it is struck, the ball shall be above the level of the playing surface and behind the server's end line, and it shall not be hidden from the receiver by any part of the body or clothing of the server or his doubles partner; as soon as the ball has been projected, the server's free arm shall be removed from the space between the server's body and the net.

1.6.5 It is the responsibility of the player to serve so that the umpire or the assistant umpire can see that he complies with the requirements for a good service.

1.6.5.1 If the umpire is doubtful of the legality of a service he may, on the first occasion in a match, declare a let and warn the server.

1.6.5.2 Any subsequent service of doubtful legality of that player or his doubles partner will result in a point to the receiver.

1.6.5.3 Whenever there is a clear failure to comply with the requirements for a good service, no warning shall be given and the receiver shall score a point.

1.6.6 Exceptionally, the umpire may relax the requirements for a good service where he is satisfied that compliance is prevented by physical disability.

1.7 A Good Return

1.7.1 The ball, having been served or returned, shall be struck so that it passes over or around the net assembly and touches the opponent's court, either directly or after touching the net assembly.

1.8 The Order of Play

1.8.1 In singles, the server shall first make a good service, the receiver shall then make a good return and thereafter server and receiver alternately shall each make a good return.

1.8.2 In doubles, the server shall first make a good service, the receiver shall then make a good return, the partner of the server shall then make a good return, the partner of the receiver shall then make a good return and thereafter each player in turn in that sequence shall make a good return.

1.9 A Let

1.9.1 The rally shall be a let

1.9.1.1 if in service the ball, in passing over or around the net assembly, touches it, provided the service is otherwise good or the ball is obstructed by the receiver or his partner;

1.9.1.2 if the service is delivered when the receiving player or pair is not ready, provided that neither the receiver nor his partner attempts to strike the ball;

1.9.1.3 if failure to make a good service or a good return or otherwise to comply with the Laws is due to a disturbance outside the control of the player;

1.9.1.4 if play is interrupted by the umpire or assistant umpire.

1.9.2 Play may be interrupted

1.9.2.1 to correct an error in the order of serving, receiving or ends;

1.9.2.2 to introduce the expedite system;

1.9.2.3 to warn or penalise a player;

1.9.2.4 because the conditions of play are disturbed in a way which could affect the outcome of the rally.

1.10 A Point

1.10.1 Unless the rally is a let, a player shall score a point

1.10.1.1 if his opponent fails to make a good service;

1.10.1.2 if his opponent fails to make a good return;

1.10.1.3 if, after he has made a good service or a good return, the ball touches anything other than the net assembly before being struck by his opponent;

1.10.1.4 if the ball passes beyond his end line without touching his court, after being struck by his opponent;

1.10.1.5 if his opponent obstructs the ball;

1.10.1.6 if his opponent strikes the ball twice successively;

1.10.1.7 if his opponent strikes the ball with a side of the racket blade whose surface does not comply with the requirements of 2.4.3, 2.4.4 and 2.4.5;

1.10.1.8 if his opponent, or anything his opponent wears or carries, moves the playing surface;

1.10.1.9 if his opponent, or anything his opponent wears or carries, touches the net assembly;

1.10.1.10 if his opponent's free hand touches the playing surface;

1.10.1.11 if a doubles opponent strikes the ball out of the sequence established by the first server and first receiver;

1.10.1.12 as provided under the expedite system (2.15.2).

1.11 A Game

1.11.1 A game shall be won by the player or pair first scoring 11 points unless both players or pairs score 10 points, when the game shall be won by the first player or pair subsequently gaining a lead of 2 points.

1.12 A Match

1.12.1 A match shall consist of the best of any odd number of games.

1.13 The Order of Serving, Receiving and Ends

1.13.1 The right to choose the initial order of serving,

receiving and ends shall be decided by lot and the winner may choose to serve or to receive first or to start at a particular end.

1.13.2 When one player or pair has chosen to serve or to receive first or to start at a particular end, the other player or pair shall have the other choice.

1.13.3 After each 2 points have been scored the receiving player or pair shall become the serving player or pair and so on until the end of the game, unless both players or pairs score 10 points or the expedite system is in operation, when the sequences of serving and receiving shall be the same but each player shall serve for only 1 point in turn.

1.13.4 In each game of a doubles match, the pair having the right to serve first shall choose which of them will do so and in the first game of a match the receiving pair shall decide which of them will receive first; in subsequent games of the match, the first server having been chosen, the first receiver shall be the player who served to him in the preceding game.

1.13.5 In doubles, at each change of service the previous receiver shall become the server and the partner of the previous server shall become the receiver.

1.13.6 The player or pair serving first in a game shall receive first in the next game of the match and in the last possible game of a doubles match the pair due to receive next shall change their order of receiving when first one pair scores 5 points.

1.13.7 The player or pair starting at one end in a game shall start at the other end in the next game of the match and in the last possible game of a match the players or pairs shall change ends when first one player or pair scores 5 points.

1.14 Out of Order of Serving, Receiving or Ends

1.14.1 If a player serves or receives out of turn, play shall be interrupted by the umpire as soon as the error is discovered and shall resume with those players serving and receiving who should be server and receiver respectively at the score that has been reached, according to the sequence established at the beginning of the match and, in doubles, to the order of serving chosen by the pair having the right to serve first in the game during which the error is discovered.

1.14.2 If the players have not changed ends when they should have done so, play shall be interrupted by the umpire as soon as the error is discovered and shall resume with the players at the ends at which they should be at the score that has been reached, according to the sequence established at the beginning of the match.

1.14.3 In any circumstances, all points scored before the discovery of an error shall be reckoned.

1.15 The Expedite System

1.15.1 Except where both players or pairs have scored at least 9 points, the expedite system shall come into operation if a game is unfinished after 10 minutes' play or at any earlier time at the request of both players or pairs.

1.15.1.1 If the ball is in play when the time limit is reached, play shall be interrupted by the umpire and shall resume with service by the player who served in the rally that was interrupted.

1.15.1.2 If the ball is not in play when the time limit is reached, play shall resume with service by the player who received in the immediately preceding rally.

1.15.2 Thereafter, each player shall serve for 1 point in turn until the end of the game and if the receiving player or pair makes 13 good returns the receiver shall score a point.

1.15.3 Once introduced, the expedite system shall remain in operation until the end of the match.

10

Tennis Psychology

The field of tennis psychology is not just common advice and tactical or mental tips. It is based on general and sports psychology and then applied to tennis specifically.

There are many common elements in the psychology of tennis which can be found in other sports too.

Thought Control

Tennis players realize how their thinking affects their body abilities and how it affects their emotions. Both body and emotions influence their tennis performance.

Our thoughts affect our body much more than we are aware of. Actually there is a part of our thinking that affects our body below our awareness.

The simplest experiment to prove this is to make a pendulum. Tie a string on a paper clip and then hold it still above the table. Then IMAGINE that the pendulum swings left and right.

You will see that it starts moving in your imagined direction without you being aware of your moving your arm. This is how our thoughts affect our body without our awareness.

Now think how this affects a game like tennis where 1 degree of racquet face change produces a difference of 40cm on the other side of the court.

Probably every tennis player has experienced a "tennis arm" where tension in our body affects our arms and legs and we feel heavy and cosntricted. This is caused by our thinking about negative consequences of an upcoming match or situation.

Obviously this tension comes from negative emotions like fear and doubt but it originates in our thinking.

You can again think how will your tennis look like in this state.

Emotion Connection

Try this – remember a painful memory and hold it i your memory for 20-30 seconds. How do you feel? Probably not good.

Now remember or imagine a happy and joyful moment and hold it for 20-30 seconds. How do you feel now?

Hopefully you are now clear on how our thoughts can create our emotions.

Now imagine, how does your tennis game look like when you are in a state of negative emotions. Your decisions are not good and your body energy is either too high or too low. More on this topic on arousal control.

A player who is not aware of his thinking just follows his thoughts and they often lead him into a negative mindset.

The goal is to become aware of his negative thinking and either change into a constructive and solution based positive one or just empty his mind. This is done with various techniques of the Inner game of Tennis.

Thought awareness is very important in peak sports performance. We can live a good and satisfying life even when we are not so vigilant about our thinking. But if we want to reach the summit in any sport then the top performers are apart by only milimetres or hundreths of a second. These small differences can be produced by our negative or incorrect thinking.

Most of amateur advice about positive thinking is good and it works well. But if you want to be a top tennis player then you need to become more and more aware of your thoughts and be able to choose what you will think.

You need to choose thoughts that will help you reach your goal and sometimes it's even better to leave your mind out of the game.

That's when you enter the zone – it's when your best abilities come out and you play your best tennis. There are no disturbing thoughts and your game just flows. And this is the final goal of thought control – no thinking at all.

How to Practice

You need to become more and more aware of what you are thinking. And hopefully you now understand how negative thinking affects your tennis and you are now motivated to change your thoughts.

1. After your practice session (and later, after the match) rate the awareness of your thoughts from 1-10. If you are totally aware of what you are thinking, then that's a 10. 1 means that whatever you think, you think automatically, and you are not able to observe your thinking. (yet)
2. Write down negative thoughts that occured to you during this practice session (or match). This will further raise your awareness.

3. Rate the ability to stop or change your negative thoughts from 1-10. 10 means that you are always able to stop and change your thinking and 1 means that your negative thoughts take over even when you are aware of what you are thinking.

Do this for one week and you will experince much higher awareness of your thinking and much higher ability to control your thinking. Stop the autopilot that you run on and choose the thoughts that make your mind your best ally.

Arousal Control

Controlling arousal enables the player to be in the ideal state

With arousal control - activation a tennis player can control his emotions and body energy – intensity. This allows him to fine tune his emotional and body state to find his ideal performance state.

Arousal or activation in this example describes the state we are in. This state is at the same time our emotional state and body energy state.

When we are over-activated it means that we are irritated, angry, upset and so on. We feel a lot of energy. That's when players throw racquets and »explode« on the court. They have too much energy for playing top tennis.

And when we are under-activated it means that we are in a bad mood, disappointed or even frustrated. This is when the energy is low and players move slowly on the court, they react too slowly and their body language shows (with low head and shoulders position) that they feel bad.

There is a so called ideal state of activation that enables us to play best tennis. This ideal state gives us a lot of energy, positive emotions (or none – just flow) and we feel enthusiastic and optimistic. We are able to react quickly and move economically and effortlessly.

Players often start the match close to this ideal state. Some of them are still under the effect of pre-match anxiety but after a while of playing tennis matches a player gets used to it.

So he starts the match close to the ideal state and then many events happen in the match which »cause« him to lose this ideal state. He gets upset, disappointed, angry, fearful and so on and he is the over- or under-activated.

Why »cause« in the brackets? Because until the player reaches acceptance about events and himself and sees reality as it is, he will feel that events are against him. He will feel cheated, that injustice has happened to him, that he shouldn't have missed a certain shot and so on. These thoughts and perceptions will make him lose his state.

When the player finds acceptance – when he accepts reality as it is, then these events cannot touch him. They are normal and the player either deals with them or let's them go.

There is one more problem in these two states beside too much or not enough body energy. We are in an emotional state and in this state we cannot think clearly. Even though we are not aware of that, the decisions that will arise and appear in our consciousness will be based on emotions.

Instead of playing a solid high cross court shot in defense we will choose to go for the corner down the line. Instead of just putting a ball away on a sitter we will hit it with full power at the line to prove something to our opponent.

In the long run this doesn't work. We make too many mistakes. We choose tactically wrong solutions; we perform our strokes under emotional influence which consequently affect our body abilities.

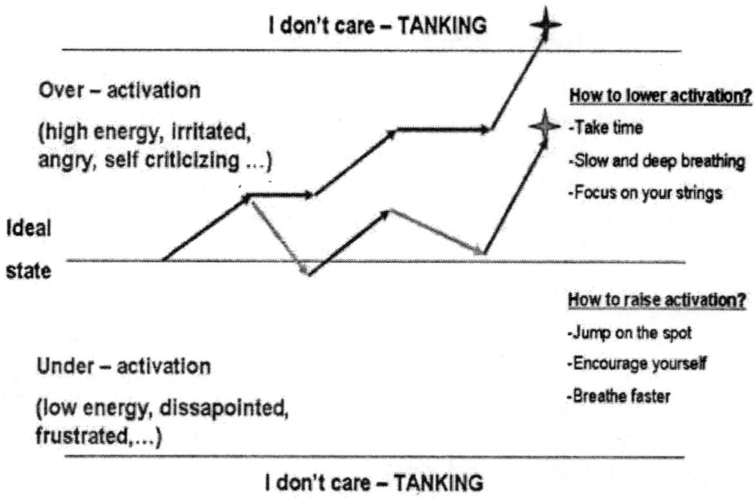

The upper diagram explains activation levels. Higher areas on the diagram mean higher activation and more energy. Lower areas on the diagram mean lower activation and less energy.

The red arrow shows how the player's activation goes up when he gets upset by his perception of an event, like a bad line call. Unless he lowers his activation (green arrow) and goes back to the ideal state, he will remain upset and on high energy.

If two more events happen that the player perceives as upsetting (wrong, shouldn't happen ..), then he will get even more activated – more energy + more powerful (and blinding) emotion (anger, rage) and possibly get over the border which I call "I don't care".

This is actually how the players say it when they've had »enough«. They don't fight anymore and are basically tanking the match. Unless some lucky coincidence helps them get down (lucky shot, opponent dropping his level of play, rain delay ..) or they calm down after some time, they will lose most of the points played.

When the player is in the "I don't care" area – state, he CANNOT be helped. His perception of tennis and life is such that he really doesn't care.

So the player must not allow himself to get there, because he will be very sorry later when thinking clearly again.

The two most common and practical ways of controlling one's arousal are on the diagram. Players need to find their own individual ways of lowering and raising their arousal which work the best for them.

How to Practice

First you have to feel the awareness of your arousal state. Then you apply the above mentioned ways of lowering or raising your arousal and see how you can do that.

1. After your practice session (or the match) rate how aware you are of your arousal state. Rate from 1 to 10.
2. Then draw the diagram of your practice or your match. Remember your ideal state, your low or your high arousal. Write down WHAT was the CAUSE and how did you play THEN.
3. Rate your ability to control arousal from 1-10. 1 means that you cannot calm down or get more energized and positive no matter what. 10 would mean that you can quickly (5-15 seconds) get back to the ideal state every time you lose your ideal state.

Practice this for one week to become more aware of your arousal and improve the ability to control your emotions and body energy.

What can a Tennis Player Control?

When a player realizes that most of the events in tennis are not under his direct control, he is able to refocus only on things that he can control.

Most of the events in any sport are not under the control of the player. Control is defined here as 100% controllable factor – like switching the light on or off. So a player cannot possibly control events like umpire calls, net cords, line shots, outside conditions like the wind, sun, noise and so on.

Another very important part out of our control is the score. Even hitting the court is not controllable. A player cannot control the score, which round in the tournament he'll reach, his ranking, whether he will win or lose ...

And what happens if the player wants to control the things that he cannot?

He becomes very anxious and tense. He wants to win this point or game but at the same time he is aware that it is not 100% certain that he will be able to do it. This desire of something that he is not sure of can cause a lot of tension inside the player's body and fight inside his mind.

This state often progresses to the state called "choking". This means that the tension and negative thinking about negative consequences are influencing the player so much, the he is unable to breathe normally (choking) and his body is very tense.

Players are usually able only to push the ball over and are unable to hit good shots. Even when they try their body doesn't listen and they almost inevitably miss.

The player must realize that this influences his play so badly that he must do his best not to get into this choking state. But as it is with everything in life, so is here – every player has experienced choking at some point in his career.

It is not something to be ashamed of or feel guilty about it. It is a normal survival response of our brain programmed inside of us for thousands of years.

Players eventually get used to these situations and also learn how to play relatively effectively even when they are under the effect of choking.

So what is the player able to control at all?

He can control his attitude and effort. He can also decide which tactical plan he will use but at the same time he needs to be aware that he cannot control the execution of this plan. Said in a more simple way – the player can decide that he will serve to the backhand of his opponent (He can control that) BUT he cannot be sure whether he will actually hit the serve in every time. (Not under his control)

The other way of explaining this is that the player needs to focus on the process and not on the end result. He can control the process – HOW but not the end result – WHAT.

He can decide to play topspin cross court shots (HOW) but not whether he will hit everyone of them in. (WHAT)

He can control that he will give his best in the third set (HOW will he play) but not whether he will win or not. (WHAT)

How to practice

The first goal for the player is to find out and get clear on what he can and what he cannot control. Take a sheet of paper and divide it in 3 columns: CAN control, CANNOT control, WHY this is not useful.

Then fill this table with the elements of the tennis match starting from the off court the day before preparation and ending after the match. For example – the player can control how much water he will drink the day before. He can also control how much time he will use for warm up before the match.

But he cannot control when he will play. If he focuses that he wants to play in the afternoon and he is not sure if that will happen, then this will cause him to be nervous and waste his physical and mental energy.

So WHY is this bad?

He is getting nervous and wasting energy instead of using it for something that he can control – like visualizing success and tactical patterns, he can take care of proper eating and drinking that will give him enough energy and enough water reserves.

Weekly practice:

1. The player first needs to become aware what elements and events of the tennis he can control and which ones he cannot. Write them down.
2. He needs to realize how this affects his game – write it down.
3. He needs to change his thinking (his focus) from the element or event that he cannot control (WHAT) to the element that he can control (HOW) and rate from 1-10 how good he is at that.

Concentration

A player becomes aware that there are more ways of

concentration and finds out which ones are the most effective in a specific situation. He learns how to concentrate and this enables him to play at his best for an extended period of time.

Concentration is one of the first sports psychology terms that athletes hear about when they start practicing their chosen sport. They often hear the coaches: "Come on, concentrate." OR "Focus now."

BUT so many players don't know the practical ways of doing that. Or maybe they try and concentrate on things that are out of their control – like winning a game – which makes them even more anxious.

There are 4 different ways of concentration which were introduced by R.M. Nideffer:

— *External wide* – when after hitting the ball the player perceives his opponent, where his ball will land, court position and so on.

— *External narrow* – when the player is about to hit the ball and his complete focus is only on the ball.

— *Internal wide* – when the player is thinking about the strategy of play before the match – tactical patterns (serve & volley, wrong footing tactics, how to play in the wind ..)

— *Internal narrow* – when the player is visualizing the serve just before the actual action.

For basic tennis psychology these different ways of concentration are not crucial. It's good to know that there are 4 main ways of concentration and that the efectiveness of the player's game is dependent on how fluidly and effectively he moves from one type to another.

The simplest and most effective ways of improving concentration are these two types:

1. emptying the mind
2. focusing on something – usually on the solution

For emptying the mind – clearing it from negative or unnecessary thoughts – a player needs to use Inner Game ways of quieting the mind. More experienced players can just stop thinking when they become aware that they are thinking too much.

When a player's mind is empty it means that he has no thoughts or words in his awareness, but that doesn't mean that he is not focused. Here is a simple demonstration: pick a small object – a pen or even a tennis ball. Throw it up in the air and catch it.

It's very probable that you were not thinking while you were watching the ball and catching it and yet you were concentrated. This is the state of having an empty mind.

Focusing on something is more useful when things don't go your way or you are having some problems. For example when you are playing in the wind your focus is on playing more away from the lines which means that you are focusing on something – your mind is not completely empty - you have a certain plan running silently in the background.

Or you play with someone with a weaker backhand and your goal is to play to that side a lot. So you are partly focusing on this task – which means that your game is not totally instinctive and yet just when you are about to hit the ball you can have a completely empty mind because you have already decided for the direction of your shot and now you just need to hit the ball cleanly.

It's important that the player looks for solutions which are automatically ways of concentrating. Staying in the problem (my backhand sucks, I'm not confident, my forehand down the line shots hit the net ..) only deepens the problem because these thoughts now make you more nervous, doubtful or angry.

Another very important point regarding concentration is that it can drop very quickly but it takes much more time to get it back up.

This diagram explains this graphically.

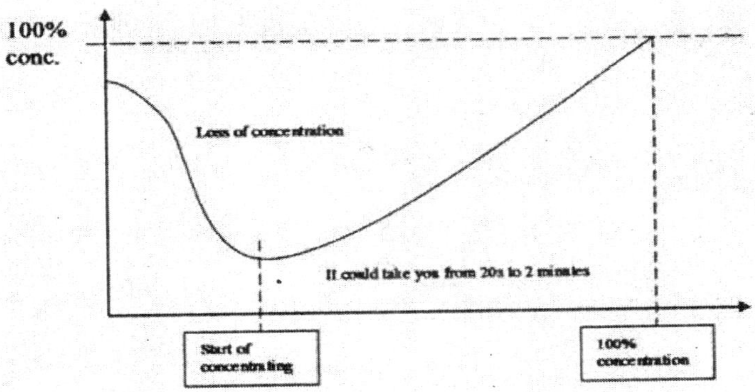

Why is this important?

When a player becomes aware that his concentration has dropped and starts building it up, it will take some time to get there.

During this time he will still not be completely focused and that can cause him to make errors.

These errors can again make the player get upset and lose concentration again. So it's important that the player realizes that he is not able to play his best tennis when he is not totally focused and that there is more chance of making a mistake.

He needs to accept these mistakes as a part of his effort of getting back to the maximum concentration. When he gets back to 100% of concentration, the number of mistakes will drop significantly.

How to practice

Write down after practice:

1. Rate the awareness of your level of concentration from 1-10. 10 means that you know when your concentration drops and 1 means that you are totally unaware of your level.
2. What events or thoughts usually cause you to lose concentration? And how does that affect your play afterwards?
3. Rate yourself from 1-10 on how good you are at concentrating – either focusing on a solution OR emptying the mind.

Visualization

One of the most powerful tools of our mind. When the player uses imagery – visualization to its fullest potential, this can accelerate his progress and help him immensely in his mental preparation of the match.

This is not some special ability that only Olympic champions use. We use it every day when we decide that we will go from point A to point B. When you decide that you want to go from one side of the city to another you visualize where you will go – which street to take, what to avoid and so on.

Tennis players also use visualization extensively but usually not in their best interest and they are not even aware what they are doing. It's when they are thinking about negative consequences of their play.

They are basically visualizing failure and feeling in the present how that will probably feel in the future. This makes them nervous, they are not focused and are expending precious energy.

They need to reverse this process and start visualizing their success and how good they will feel when they achieve it. This will fill them with lots of positive energy and program them for success.

Where can visualization be used in the game of tennis?

It can be used in all four major areas of tennis:

1. *Technique* – when the player is still learning a new stroke or improving an existing one, he first needs to see the correct execution on the video or in demonstration and then visualize how he performs this stroke perfectly. This will greatly speed up the learning process.
2. *Tactics and strategy* – when the player is planning his strategy before the match he can visualize how he hits certain combinations of shots. He can visualize good and precise serving, returning and all other areas of the tennis match. When he plays he will react and decide much faster because he will already have preprogrammed decisions and directions.
3. *Physical abilities* – the same as athletes visualize how they jump higher or longer, so can a tennis player visualize how fast he is, how is he able to withstand fatigue and how strong he is in the third set. Mental images have incredible influence on our bodies when we use them consistently.
4. *Mental preparation* – the most effective way of visualizing in the mental area is when the player imagines how he plays the finals or in front of many people. It happens many times that the player gets

nervous before or at the beginning of an important match because he is not used to pressure around him.

If he visualizes these situations before, he gets used to them in his mind and when they happens in reality he is ready and relaxed.

Another very effective way of using visualization is when the player anticipates situations in the match that could potentially cause him to lose focus or to get upset. He then visualizes these situations and how he handles them. That way he prepares for when they happen in reality and he immediately knows how to respond because of the previous programming in his mind.

How to visualize effectively

— Sit comfortably in your chair and take a couple of deep breaths to relax first. Then put yourself in your mind on the tennis court and try to see the colors.

— Next try to see the shapes of the objects on the court – the net, the chair, the fence...

— Then try and hear the sounds that you would normally hear on the court – the sound of hitting the ball, your breathing and other sounds.

— Then try and feel your movement and your strokes. Make a forehand topspin in your mind and try to feel how that would really feel. Then try to feel your movement on the court from left to right and so on.

— The last and most important component are your emotions. This time try to feel the emotions of how good you would feel if you hit a certain shot, won a match or reached your desired ranking.

— When you include your positive emotions: joy, enthusiasm, happiness and satisfaction, then the effect of visualization is much more profound and permanent.

Another very effective and useful use of visualization is immediately after you make an error on the court. As soon as you miss, you turn away and in your mind see how the ball hit the target. See it exactly – how high over the net, where on the court and how fast and with how much spin you played it.

This has double effect – it takes you away of your negative thinking since you are not seeing success and it also trains your body for the next similar situation when you will have to play a similar shot. This way it will be already stored in your mind.

One final, very important use of visualization is explained in the Mental Manual for Tennis Winners. It explains why when we analyze the match and learn what went wrong again make the same mistakes in our next match. It also explains how to use visualization to avoid making the same mistakes over and over again.

How to practice

Practice for one week the following ways of visualization:

1. After you make an error imagine how you actually hit the ball. Write down some of the mistakes and how you imagined them later.
2. Rate yourself from 1-10 how good you are at this – 10 means that you can do it clearly and immediately, 1 means that you can't do it and that you don't see anything (yet)
3. Every night before you fall asleep visualize for 5 minutes one of the elements of the tennis game that you want to improve – technique, tactical play, physical or mental abilities.

There is a lot of chance that after only one week of practice you may see significant results. Be open to this possibility.

Self Confidence

If you want to build self confidence, you must first find out what it actually is. It is a belief – trust – faith the player has about him being able to complete a task in the future successfully. He trusts in himself and his abilities which he perceives to be good enough to overcome the problem – challenge.

If the player looks to build confidence, then we must first discover the reasons why he hasn't any self confidence. There are 4 main reasons for that:

1. He hasn't done anything worth any good value. Self confident people are those with good results – with notable achievements. This is the first step to a true and deep feeling of confidence which is based on real facts – results.

2. If the player has done a good job – practicing hard and with 100% effort, has developed good sound technique, understands the game well and plays a tactically smart game and he thinks that all that is nothing or not very good, than he will not be confident about himself.

   Many players are too critical about themselves or some parts of their game. They see mistakes which may be there, but there are also many good points that the player has but doesn't notice them.

   Many are also too focused on fixing "wrong" things instead of "improving" their already good things that will eventually make the "wrong" things disappear.

   For example: if you hit the ball long you can then try to: - not to hit the ball wrong – fixing the problem- Or try to hit the ball in – improving on the good point

3. Players focus too much on winning, which is not under their control. For some players only a win means that they are good. If they lose, they lose also their feeling of self confidence.
4. The last reason for not being really self confident about himself is the foundation of self confidence – self esteem. It is the feeling and measure of self worth in general. If the player thinks about himself that he is no one special, that he has many flaws, he is not really a worthy person, then these feelings and beliefs influence his tennis self confidence too.

Then what is the opposite of self confidence?

It is doubt! Doubt is actually a series of questions that we ask ourselves and then reply with NO. The graphical presentation will make this clearer.

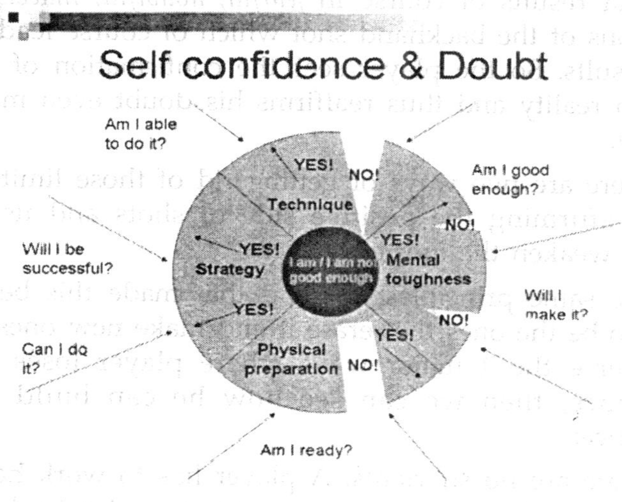

Most sports (and tennis included) have 4 main areas that a player needs to master in order to be a top player:

technique, strategy and tactics, physical preparation and mental preparation – toughness.

Every player has some weaknesses in some areas – which are represented in the upper diagram as white areas – holes. This is where his answer will be "no", the constant doubting questions that appear in his mind.

Unfortunately, this is not the whole problem about the lack of self confidence. The biggest problem for the player are his perceptions of what he is good at, which skills he masters and in which areas he can rely on himself.

The player may have a technically excellent backhand and can play every possible type of shot with it with good consistency, but his belief is that his backhand is poor. So even though in reality his backhand is good (he has no »holes« in that area) he believes that his backhand is poor (perceives a "hole").

That results of course in *fearful, doubtful, indecisive* executions of the backhand shot which of course lead to poor results. So the player sees the confirmation of his belief in reàlity and thus reaffirms his doubt even more strongly.

There are two ways of getting rid of those limiting beliefs: affirming the positive side of shots and using logic to weaken the limiting belief.

The same principles of mind that made this belief will also be the ones that erase it and make new ones. If we reverse the 4 major ways where player loses his confidence, then we can see how he can build his confidence:

1. There are no shortcuts. A player has to work hard, has to be focused and persistent to be at least solid if not very good in all areas of the tennis game. He must work on all his weaknesses to eliminate all "holes" where doubt can cling on.

2. The player needs to be aware of what he does well. This is crucial and the most important aspect of building self confidence. Even though he may be focused on a weakness which he is working on he must be alert and ready to see every good shot that he makes.
3. He must also get very clear on what elements he can control and focus on those. He cannot control winning and he must not allow his self confidence to depend on winning. He needs to focus on his best effort, how he fought with all the circumstances and never gave up. This is what gives deep and solid confidence.
4. Last but not least – he needs to be successful in other areas of life. He must value himself as a worthy human being who is also a nice person, someone that people can trust and rely on, and someone who is successful in career, relationships and general life skills. This is the foundation of his self worth which affects his tennis specific self confidence.

How to Practice (improve)

Every day after practice write this down:

1. 3 things that you did really good today – and have at least one of them psychological (for example: I was totally concentrated for 10 minutes, I didn't get angry because of a missed sitter, ..)
2. Which weakness did you work on today? What improvement did you notice (it can be very small, just see it.)
3. What other improvements of the 4 main areas of the game did you notice today?

If you are diligent with this practice and write down every day just 3 positive things about your game, you'll have 15 positive thoughts about your game in just 5 days. That will reach 60 in one month.

If you then read these positive statements, which are not some out of the air affirmations but your actual notes, then you will feel a great deal of self confidence which will represent your inner strength. No coach or parent told you these positive things about your game – they are yours. And this is true SELF confidence.

BELIEFS

An athlete that holds many limiting beliefs limits his own success. When he realizes that these beliefs are false, he is free to perform at his peak regardless of circumstances or his abilities – positive and negative ones. Beliefs are ways of thinking for which we believe that are true. Every person has a certain logic and proof that his belief is true. Unfortunately, many of these beliefs are harmful and limiting for one's success and improvement.

Some typical limiting beliefs of tennis players are:

— every time things start to go my way bad things start to happen

— the last game is the hardest one

— if I lose my advantage (leading 5:2 in the set, 40:0 in a game), I am a loser

— good players don't make stupid mistakes. I made a "stupid" mistake therefore I'm not a good player. Bad players cannot win tournaments or tough matches

— he gets all the luck, never me

Many of the beliefs are subconscious. The player only sees that his game falls apart at certain critical situations in the match but doesn't know where those feelings of fear or doubt come from.

Only with detailed analysis of his thinking and logic can he discover the underlying limiting belief.

When the player becomes aware of his beliefs, he is half way to free himself of them. With a realistic view on sport and himself a player becomes open to all events that happen during a match. He is in a state of acceptance.

To really become free of beliefs a player needs to find out that they are not true. He can do that with logical thinking and with realistic observation of other players, tennis matches and various situations that happen in a tennis match.

For example – a player may be convinced (belief) that his serve is really bad and that he made many double faults. This is how his belief filters all the information and lets in the memory only events that are proving and reinforcing the belief.

If a player then watches a video tape of his match and makes a detailed statistics of his serving, he may discover that he made 3 double faults but he also put 26 second serves in. That's around 90% of the second serve success.

And out of those 26 second serves he actually forced 7 times a short return which he could then put away with a winner.

He can then compare his stats with top players in his league or even with top ATP players and then set realistic beliefs about his serve.

Why are beliefs problematic?

If a player has a belief that his second serve is weak, he will feel insecure and fearful almost every time he serves a second serve. Our thinking and emotions heavily influence our ability to perform at our best.

Another common way of limiting beliefs is that some things shouldn't happen. This causes the player to become stressed, emotional and lose his focus. His level of playing drops.

The most typical events that shouldn't happen are:

- lucky net cord from his opponent
- line shots
- bad line calls
- getting aced by a bad server
- the opponent hitting a winner because of a mishit shot

But the reality is that all these events have happened, do happen and will happen again. What players hold in their mind is an illusionary fairy tale of how nice the matches should unfold. Once they get real and are ready to deal with anything that happens they are in a state of acceptance.

Acceptance means that everything that happens is perfectly normal. It just happened, so that's the way it is. Acceptance doesn't mean resigning to fate. Resigning to fate means that you don't do anything against events that happen. Acceptance means that you do everything in your power against events that happen and still accept that you cannot control reality.

Things sometimes do not go your way. Most of the time players think about an easier way. They cannot comprehend that a real tennis match can be so tough. Some of the players are too afraid to deal with reality because sometimes events in the match can make it really hard for one to come through. That's called growing – as a tennis player and as a person.

When a player accepts himself and all the events, he is free from negative thoughts or thinking how things should be. His mind is calm and clear. He can play his best tennis. How to discover and get rid of limiting beliefs

Read these statements and see what you come up with after the first part:

— If I lose my lead (5:2 to 5:5, 40:0 to 40:40, ..) it means that...

— I lost my match because of:

  — one mistake at the beginning (Yes/No)

  — a double fault when I served for the set (Yes/No)

  — bad luck (Yes/No)

  — If I make mistakes then...

  — Since I played badly last time (yesterday, this week, ..) I will play badly today (Yes/No)

These are some of the beliefs that we commonly hold for true.

— Take your time this week and attentively listen to your friends, coaches, TV or radio to identify more beliefs about tennis or anything else.

— You can discover your personal beliefs by first identifying situations where you perform below your best. Maybe it is serving for the match, maybe it is playing in the finals, and maybe it is playing against someone specific.

— When you find the recurring situation try and remember what you think when it happens. What are you trying to avoid when being in that situation? What will give you most emotional pain if things that you don't want to experience happen?

What does that tell about you?

After you have found your beliefs ask yourself the following questions:

1. Is that true? Can you find any proof that exactly the opposite is true?
2. Is this in my best interest?
3. Does this type of thinking make my journey towards my goal easier or more difficult?
4. Does this type of thinking lead me to my goal at all or am I going away from reaching my goal?

Once you realize with logical thinking that your belief is not true and that it does not work for you, you can either choose a new one that will help you or just accept events as they unfold. If you are in a state of acceptance, events don't bother you. You are focused on your goal even when unwanted events happen. You can use the following demonstration to experience acceptance:

Place a tennis ball 20 feet away from you on the ground and take 5 or 6 tennis balls in your hands. Now throw each one and try to hit that tennis ball on the ground. Just throw the balls one after another and try to hit the ball.

Regardless of the outcome, ask yourself:

— Did you try any less when you missed the ball?

— Did you try much harder when you missed?

— Did you criticize yourself when you missed?

— What do you think about mistakes that happened?

Most people do not get angry or do not see their mistakes as mistakes. They see them as feedback. You are accepting mistakes as part of the task, not your deficiency or inferiority or anything like that.

Write down for one week after your practice:

1. Did you recognize any beliefs – your own or someone else's?
2. Check with yourself whether:

— is that true?
— does that way of thinking help you?
— how does that affect your future effort and commitment?

3. Have you recognized any differences in beliefs that people have about the same event or circumstance? Can you see that there are many ways of describing the same situation?

Once you expose your beliefs and see them as unlogical you are free and all possibilities are open. You are not limited by your thinking.

Develop a still mind and enter the zone

The Inner Game of Tennis approach is based on this simple idea – the key to peak performance lies in the mind of the player. This approach is extensively described in the Inner Game section, so here we present only practical applications of the three fundamentals:

To experience a quiet mind:

— Pick a small object, throw it in the air and catch it. During the flight of this object your mind was empty. There were no thoughts. There may be some if you repeat the exercise since now you are aware of what is happening.

— The goal of quieting the mind is to focus it on something and thus prevent thinking which disturbs the mind body connection.

To experience trusting the body:

— If you stand on one leg and become aware of all the muscles in your leg, you'll notice that they work all the time to keep you in balance. The more aware you are, the more you'll feel how your muscles move – contract and expand.

— And yet, this is not what you're doing consciously.

— You can consciously move your body if you want to and those movements are the result of Self1 commands. But when you compare these movements with those in your leg when you are holding balance, you'll see a big difference.

— The movements in your leg are subconscious – made by the body or Self.

To experience non-judgment:

— The simplest experiment is to try and hit a small target (tennis ball) on the ground about 20 feet away from you. Throw tennis balls and try to hit the target.

Then ask yourself:

— Did you criticize yourself when you missed?

— Did you have any negative thoughts about yourself or your abilities?

Probably not. You were in the state of non-judgment. This exercise helps you experience that you can perform tasks and be non-judgmental about yourself. That way you are totally focused on the task.

How to practice

Every day after practice:

1. Where in today's practice or match did you experience that Self2 made corrections instead of you?
2. Do you remember having a still mind? Being totally focused on the task and having no thoughts run through your awareness?
3. Did you make any mistakes and didn't judge

yourself? That means that you accepted them as a normal part of the game or yourself.

4. How did you play afterwards, when you accepted the errors? How do you play when you don't accept them? Will reality ever change?

After you have gone through these questions for one week you'll have much higher awareness of the inner game principles and you'll be ready to trust them. You'll know when Self1 will start talking to you and you'll know that you don't need to listen to it.

How to Overcome the Fear of Losing

Many tennis players are pressured by the fear of losing when they play a match. But when they practice or play a practice match, none of this fear is present. But the fear of losing usually isn't the fear of losing a tennis match.

Losing a tennis match is not a big deal. It means only that someone else played better than you. You may feel uncomfortable about that, because you are disappointed in the result of this test of your tennis skills. But if you don't connect your tennis skill with how you feel about yourself (as being worthy, being a good person, and so forth), then losing a tennis match is really not a big deal.

It's really the CONSEQUENCES of losing a tennis match that you fear. The negative consequences of losing a tennis match stay buried in your subconscious, and you think that you are afraid of losing a match, when you are actually afraid of the consequences of losing a match.

There is another angle to the consequences:

1. You can be afraid of present and realistic negative consequences. For example: if you lose, you won't get the prize money and be able to afford a flight home. Or, if you lose, you won't get points for the Wimbledon first round of juniors.

2. You can also be afraid of past pain, pain you experienced in a previous loss. For example: when you were 10 years old and lost a match, your father scolded you or hit you.

Consequences and How can you Solve

The first approach has to do with the consequences that happen now, in which the emotional pain is not based on past painful events.

You need to make all the possible negative consequences conscious by writing them down and then imagining that each of them do happen.

Really get into the story of losing a match and how your worst fears come true, like your friends make fun of you, your opponents ridicule you in the locker room, you lose rankings, and so on.

And then you need to ask two things:

1. What is the probability of this actually happening?
2. If it happens, can I handle it? Will I survive? Will life go on?

Note that the mind has an unbelievable ability to create horror stories even when there is almost no chance of those events actually happening. The only way to challenge the mind's ability to create fiction is to go with the story, setting it against reality and facts.

Ninety-nine percent of the time, you realize that the fear of losing is empty and dismiss it as unrealistic. That's when your negative mind starts losing power over you. Because you don't believe it anymore. The first and hardest step in this process is realizing that it is not you doing the thinking: it is the mind.

And it is you who must make a conscious choice whether to follow the thought or dismiss it as unrealistic and unhelpful in achieving your goals. In cases where the negative consequences are real, you must accept them. That is, you must be willing to endure the negative consequences of losing a match.

The mind can make you view these negative consequences as horrible so that you lose perspective of what "horrible" really is. Those are truly horrible things.

In other words, just get a realistic perspective on what feeling bad and suffering are. Your goal is to be 100% sure that you want to play and that you accept the possibility of losing and all the consequences that go along with losing. Only then will you be free to play unburdened.

As long as there is a tiny part of you not accepting the negative consequences of losing, you will be nervous and unable to fully concentrate on the match. In other words, some part of your mind will be pulling against you instead of with you in the direction of winning and going for it.

Why? Because going for it increases the chances of losing and experiencing pain. For better understanding, let's imagine an extreme situation: someone has kidnapped your child. (or any loved one – another horrible situation)

They will return the child safely to you if:

— you drink 1 liter of sea water (which is very unpleasant)

— eat one ounce of sand (ditto)

— roll your self in manure

— go into the mall like that to buy groceries

— and walk naked on the street.

So there are some humiliating and extremely distasteful things one might have to do in life, but would you hesitate to do them in order to bring back your child safely?

No, not even for a second.

You would accept these consequences even though they are unwanted events that make you suffer.

Losing a tennis match is most likely to be less painful. But you must completely accept the possible consequences if you want to be 100% focused and determined to reach your goal.

Only then will your mind support you and become your ally.

Fear of Losing and Past Emotional Pain

The other approach has to with you having subconscious pain associated with losing or missing a shot in the past. This emotional pain stays in your subconscious (since it wasn't resolved), and now any similar event triggers fear of similar pain, which you will try to avoid.

In fact, one of the mind's main purposes is to protect us from pain. It does so by comparing current circumstances to past circumstances that led to pain. If the mind notices a similarity (and it takes very safe margins) between them, it alerts you and tries to make you avoid these circumstances.

When we talk about tennis, it means that you enter a tournament, and there is some past pain associated with playing tournaments. You lost a tournament match before and suffered much emotional pain. So now whenever you enter a tournament your mind warns you that doing this might cause pain and sends signals making you feel very uncomfortable (nervous, anxious, doubtful, and so on), pressing you to decide to avoid this situation. But since you cannot just quit the tournament and you have consciously decided to play it, your mind is now split – you want to play and you don't want to play.

This ambivalence creates tension in your mind. Consequently you cannot play well. And since you don't play well, you probably lose. And so the whole cycle starts again. The prediction of experiencing pain in tournaments is now reinforced in your mind. Therefore, next time it sends even stronger signals to make you avoid playing a tournament. It makes you even more nervous, thus preventing you from playing your best and thus causing the very thing it wants to avoid.

11

Physiological Demands in Tennis

The physiological demands of tennis and how a player's body responds to meet these demands are not as clearly understood as they are for some other sports and activities. Tennis is characterized by intermittent bouts of activity of variable intensities and durations. Moreover, the length of a match can be less than an hour to more than four hours.

Tennis can also be played on a variety of surfaces with a wide range of accompanying environmental conditions. All of these factors play a significant role in defining the energy demands on the body and how a player must physiologically respond. Understanding these perspectives are important to a coach, so that s/he can help any player to appropriately and optimally train, compete and recover from play.

Many of the physiological processes related to play involve converting stored chemical energy to mechanical energy to in order to run, hit the ball, and recover. In addition, after each one of these bouts of muscular activity, the chemical energy in the muscles must be rapidly restored.

These processes go on throughout a match and a player's ability to continue playing depend in large part on one's physiological capacity to efficiently and rapidly convert, utilize, and replenish energy as it is needed. This can become a great challenge as a match get goes on and the intensity of play increases. Moreover, as body temperature goes up, energy replacement and effective utilization becomes even more difficult.

One of the key components to maintaining optimal energy conversion and restoration throughout a match (i.e., endurance) is a player's ability to take in and utilize oxygen. With a high aerobic capacity, the cardiovascular system is able to deliver oxygen effectively. Muscles will also adapt to be able to utilize oxygen more efficiently and rapidly. Thereby, a player can continue to play longer without fatiguing as rapidly or having to reduce the intensity of play as much. This, combined with the body's ability to provide energy to the muscles at a very high rate to maintain power, speed, and strength (via adaptations of other physiological systems), will give a player a tremendous advantage over one who is less physiologically well trained and conditioned.

Energy Demand

The body has three systems that continually function together to provide the energy needed for muscle activity and replenish energy stores. These are the immediate, non-oxidative glycolysis, and oxidative metabolic systems. The former are considered as anaerobic (not dependent on oxygen) energy systems and the third refers to the body's aerobic (in the presence of oxygen) energy system. All three are important during tennis play.

ATP – The Energy Building Block

The immediate source of energy for all muscle contractions is a chemical called adenosine triphosphate (ATP). ATP is a high-energy molecule that stores a considerable amount of energy within the chemical bonds that hold the molecule together. The energy needed for muscle contraction is produced when an ATP molecule is broken down into adenosine diphosphate (ADP) and phosphate. Typically, for ADP to be "recharged," so that it can produce more energy, the ADP and phosphate must be chemically reattached to reform ATP. The three energy system described below all function to replenish the ATP stores in a muscle.

Immediate Energy System

As ATP is used, another chemical called creatine phosphate (CP) is available to be broken down (into creatine and phosphate) to almost immediately replenish a muscles' ATP supply. The ongoing processes of ATP breakdown and restoration of ATP by the separation of CP are anaerobic – in other words no oxygen is required for, or directly involved in, either of these processes. The CP system is used to fuel short, intense activities that last for several seconds or so. The CP reserve is about 5-6 times that of ATP, so a player has plenty of CP to effectively restore energy (ATP) during most points and movements on the court. One molecule of ATP is reformed for every molecule of CP that is broken down.

The CP system is very effective and sufficient process for meeting the short-term energy demands of tennis. However, to keep going, the assistance of two other energy-providing systems is needed. Moreover, these other support energy systems are relied on as well to restore muscle energy during and between points when the demand for energy in a given muscle or muscle group is less.

Non-oxidative Glycolysis

Carbohydrate, in the form of glucose or glycogen (stored

form in the liver or muscles) can be biochemically broken down to provide energy in the form of ATP via a process called glycolysis. This energy system is also an anaerobic system and does not require the presence of oxygen to create ATP. The fast glycolytic system provides most of the energy for activities lasting up to 2 minutes. The CP system, as mentioned, provides the initial burst of energy in any activity. However, if the demand for muscle energy requires ATP to be provided at a fast rate for a longer period of time, then the fast-glycolytic system will be used. Using the fast-glycolysis system, a molecule of glucose is used to produce 2 molecules of ATP.

This system is also sometimes referred to as the lactic acid system, since lactate is a byproduct of this form of metabolism. This energy system might be used when a player runs hard from side to side in order to hit a series of ground strokes. If the duration and intensity of points continues to increase (or stay high), then the proportionate reliance on this lactic acid producing system increases. Even though the oxidative (aerobic) metabolism system will also function to provide energy to working muscles, the rate of ATP production via aerobic metabolism is not fast enough to keep up with this temporary high demand.

Fortunately, such a high demand is not usually sustained for very long periods of time. If it did, then a high level of lactic acid would accumulate in the muscles and fatigue would set in quickly. Because, tennis is so intermittent and a repeated high demand in a given group of muscles occurs so irregularly and infrequently, the lactic acid level in a tennis player during play rarely gets very high.

Oxidative Metabolism

As effective as the immediate and non-oxidative

glycolysis systems are for providing rapid energy during tennis, the oxidative (aerobic) metabolism system can supply substantially more energy and plays a critical role throughout play. As an example, each molecule of glucose that is broken down by aerobic metabolism produces 38 molecules of ATP. Carbohydrate, fat, and even protein can be used to fuel aerobic metabolism. Use of these nutrients to provide energy via the utilization of oxygen will lessen the burden on glycolysis alone and thus a player will be able to provide and restore energy for a much longer period before feeling the effects of carbohydrate depletion or lactic acid accumulation. Again, even when the intensity of play is high and anaerobic glycolysis is called upon to meet the greater muscle energy demand, oxidative metabolism continues at the same time.

When the intensity of a point is lessened (and certainly between those hard points), aerobic metabolism is already working to rapidly help the muscle cells to recover. A sufficient aerobic capacity will help a player to recover faster – during and between points. Overall, the aerobic (oxidative) metabolism system is the primary source of ATP production and energy restoration during a tennis match – even though the other anaerobic (non-oxidative) systems are continually functioning as well.

Aerobic Training

Despite the intermittent nature of tennis, continuous singles play (i.e., without a lot of extended breaks and rest periods) can provide, in itself, a cardiorespiratory conditioning effect, if one plays often and regularly enough. This not only yields an increase in a player's aerobic power (capacity), but there can be myriad other beneficial physiological adaptations as well that could enhance performance and reduce certain health risks (e.g., lower body fat, enhanced heart efficiency, lower blood pressure, and enhanced blood lipid profile). However, to meet the on-court physiological demands and develop the level of aerobic fitness required of today's high-level players, a certain amount of supplemental aerobic conditioning is often necessary.

There is a wide array of on- and off-court exercises that will enhance a player's aerobic capacity (endurance). Endurance training can include moderate- to high-volume, interval or continuous, on- or off-court tennis-specific drills, as well as the more traditional forms of distance running and cycling. The key to enhancing the aerobic system is keeping the heart rate elevated for a fairly long time (either continuous or with higher intensity intervals and short rest periods between).

Generally, the player should keep the intensity below the lactic acid threshold (or the intensity when the aerobic system can not meet the player's energy needs and more energy is produced via fast-glycolysis). In other words, you do not want to go so hard that your body has to rely on anaerobic glycolysis to a great degree, where you end up producing a lot of lactic acid. Breathing rate (if it is too high) can be an indicator or crossing the anaerobic threshold.

However, monitoring heart rate is usually a more effective way, especially without having the option of using more sophisticated measuring tools. You and your players need to be able to monitor training intensities to ensure that the aerobic energy system is the one being primarily and sufficiently stimulated and stressed. Whether you use a high-tech heart rate monitor or simply feel the radial (wrist) or carotid (neck) pulse, simply monitoring heart rate can give you and your players invaluable information about exercise intensity.

The recommended range for heart rate during an activity to promote aerobic fitness is between approximately 60 and 85% of the individual's maximum heart rate. Despite the variability in maximal heart rate within specific age ranges, the following formula can be used to estimate one's heart rate range for enhancing aerobic fitness:

— (220 – age of player) x .60 = lowest heart rate (60%)

— (220 – age of player) x .85 = highest heart rate (85%)

For example, a 20-year-old player would want to train at an intensity where his or her heart rate would be between 120 and 170 beats per minute. Keep in mind, when you are training in the heat, there is usually a compensatory increase in heart rate, due to the body having to maintain cardiac output while regulating temperature at the same time. In addition, such training should occur several times a week for a duration of at least 20-30 minutes each time, depending on a player's current fitness and aerobic enhancement goals.

Anaerobic Training

Anaerobic exercise is characterized by brief, high-intensity periods of activity, where energy metabolism during the activity periods is predominantly provided by the systems that do not involve oxygen. Anaerobic training would include a series of these activities, each one followed by a specified period of rest to allow for replenishment of the anaerobic energy stores within the working muscles. Such exercises can include a variety of high-intensity, short-duration activities on the court or a variety of running drills/sprints at a track or open field.

The work-to-rest ratio does not have to mimic that of tennis (e.g., 10 seconds on, 25-30 seconds off). In fact, just like with aerobic conditioning, to get the body to adapt in ways beyond what tennis in itself would do (i.e., enhance anaerobic capacity and tolerance further), a player needs to extend beyond the demands that would be encountered on the court (i.e., overload).

For example, high intensity running intervals could range from 2 seconds to 30 seconds. Just keep in mind that the longer the activity (work) interval is, the longer the recovery (rest) interval should be. Also keep in mind that the higher the intensity, the more repeated exercises you perform, and the shorter the rest intervals are – the greater demand there is on the body. As important and beneficial as anaerobic interval training can be for helping to optimally develop a tennis player, such training is very demanding. Without sufficient preparation, progression (within the session and over longer periods of time), warm-up, and recovery, too much of this type of training can readily lead to injury.

Activities that can be used to enhance a player's anaerobic capacity could include:

— Wind sprints
— Line drills
— Spider drill
— Alley hops
— Side shuffles
— Cariocas
— Ladder drills
— Split-step progressions
— Hexagon drill
— Circuit training

Flexibility Training (Streching)

One of the most misunderstood training modes in most players' programs is stretching. Having tennis players stretch not only can prevent injuries but also can enhance performance. Flexibility is simply defined as the ability of the body's muscles and soft tissue to elongate or lengthen to allow movement around a joint. The two primary forms of stretching are static and dynamic, both of which can be used effectively and safely by tennis players. Other types of stretching include proprioceptive neuromuscular facilitation and ballistic stretching.

Static Stretching

Static stretching is one of the safest and most effective forms of stretching. It has been used by athletes for many years and has been proven to increase muscle length and motion of the joints. Characteristics of static stretches include the following:

— The body is positioned to isolate a muscle or group of muscles.

— Slow, controlled movements are used.

— A period of holding or static posturing is used to stretch the muscle at its end range or near the limit of available motion.

Static stretching typically is done in a particular sequence that has been found to enhance the muscles' ability to elongate:

— Perform a general body warm-up prior to performing static stretching. This can be doing light calisthenics, riding a cycle, or jogging slowly around the court until a very light sweat appears.

— Perform static stretches using positions that safely place a muscle or muscle group in an elongated position.

— Hold the stretch for approximately 15 to 30 seconds. Research has not demonstrated any benefit to holds longer than 30 seconds, nor have periods of stretching less than 10 seconds produced effective tissue lengthening.

— Repeat the stretch.

While recent research has brought into question the effectiveness of static stretching immediately before a sport or explosive movement (such as running or jumping at maximum intensity), sports medicine professionals still endorse the use of static stretching due to its ability to improve muscles' flexibility. Whenever possible, players should stretch both before and especially after exercise training or tennis play/competition. Stretching the muscles after exercise or tennis play helps to minimize the post-exercise soreness and stiffness players often encounter after a hard workout or lengthy match.

Stretching should become a regular part of the players' training program. An evaluation by a sports medicine professional can assist players in identifying areas that need particular attention in their stretching programs, with regular testing and evaluation being an important part of any player's long-range development.

Dynamic Stretching

Dynamic stretching is a form of stretching that is used to prepare the body's musculature for specific activities. Instead of specific postures and static positions, dynamic stretching actually uses sport-specific movement patterns, which are typically performed after a general warm-up, such as riding a stationary bike. The movements used in a dynamic stretching routine can be actual tennis strokes, jogging in place, side-to-side shuffles, butt kicks, or movements mimicking actual tennis movement patterns.

The idea behind dynamic stretching exercises is to warm up the body and raise a player's core temperature. At the same time, these exercises move muscles and joints through movement patterns that actually will be encountered during the sport activity. This prepares the muscles and joints for the stresses of the game.

Flexibility programs typically incorporate both static and dynamic flexibility exercises, as in this example:

— Warm-up

— Dynamic stretches

— Sport activity

— Static stretches after sport activity

Proprioceptive Neuromuscular Facilitation (PNF)

An advanced concept in stretching that is now used by many coaches and trainers is proprioceptive neuromuscular facilitation (PNF). This type of stretching uses a partner and involves contracting and relaxing a muscle or muscle group to elicit a greater stretch. During this type of stretching the athlete is actually contracting the muscle isometrically near the end of the available movement pattern, then subsequently relaxing it as the partner moves the limb farther into the stretch pattern. Here are the steps you would take as a partner in this type of stretching:

— Take the limb to right near the end of the available range of motion.

— Ask the player to isometrically contract the muscle for up to 6 seconds as you are stretching and to resist any movement during the contraction.

— Have the player relax the muscle, then slowly move the limb farther in the direction you are trying to stretch for 15 to 30 seconds.

— Repeat the sequence.

The theory behind this type of stretching is that a period of deeper muscle relaxation occurs immediately following a contraction of that muscle. Neurologically speaking, the muscle will best be able to relax after it has been stimulated or asked to contract. This method of stretching takes advantage of this relaxation period to obtain a better stretch of the muscle or muscle group. It can be particularly effective for players who are having difficulty with a particular muscle group or who find it very difficult to relax their muscles while stretching.

Ballistic Stretching

One type of stretch that is not recommended is the ballistic stretch. Ballistic stretches involve fast, sudden movements at the end of a joint's range of movement that are intended to improve flexibility. While some sources report improvement using ballistic stretches, doing this type of stretch increases the chances of injury. Safer forms of static and dynamic stretches that use smoother, less jerky movements without bouncing are preferable.

Strength Training

You will be better able to assist players with their strength training programs if you understand several key concepts: the types of muscle contractions, the body's adaptations to strength training, how to determine the appropriate resistance level for strength training, and overload and progression.

Types of Contractions

Muscular contractions occur in three main forms: isometric, concentric, and eccentric.

Isometric muscular contractions occur when the muscle contracts but no joint movement occurs. Such contractions are used by the body to stabilize joints; but, as no joint motion is produced, they are not used to move body segments. Tennis players can perform isometric training as part of their training programs, but it is not considered very useful, as tennis requires complex movements and is a very dynamic activity.

Concentric muscular contractions occur when the muscle fibers actually shorten. This produces a shortening movement between where the muscle originates (starts) and inserts (ends, attaching to a bone). An example of a concentric muscular contraction would be the action of the bicep muscle during an arm curl exercise as the weight is brought up toward the shoulder or face. Concentric muscular contractions are typically used during the acceleration of body segments. For example, when the arm is accelerating forward during a serve, muscles in the front of the body, such as the pectorals, are contracting concentrically.

Eccentric muscular contractions occur when muscle fibers lengthen. This allows the body to decelerate or break a segment. For example, during the arm curl exercise mentioned earlier, the bicep muscle works eccentrically as the weight is lowered from the shoulder. If we were unable to perform eccentric contractions, the body would be unable to slowly control the lowering of a weight or object and uncontrolled shaky movements would occur. In tennis, eccentric contractions are used by the muscles in the back of the shoulder such as the rhomboids and rotator cuff during the follow-through phase of the serve (following ball impact) to slow the arm and maintain joint integrity and control. In general, eccentric contractions are thought to be stabilizing contractions that serve to absorb force and decelerate body segments.

Eccentric contractions are harder on the body than concentric contractions in terms of the stress imparted to tissue. While a person perceives that he or she is working less while walking down a steep hill or into the Grand Canyon, the muscle fibers and the structures around them are actually being stressed to a greater degree than when the individual is walking up a hill or out of the Grand Canyon. It is important to keep this in mind, as excessive eccentric muscle work can lead to extreme muscle soreness. This soreness typically presents itself 36 to 72 hours after exercise and has been termed delayed onset muscle soreness (DOMS). For this reason, eccentric training is usually used in a more limited fashion and combined with concentric muscle training to minimize the effects from delayed onset muscle soreness.

Contraction Guidelines

Strength training is an important component of a complete conditioning program for a tennis player, and it can greatly enhance performance when applied correctly. Here are a few general recommendations for training:

— Use both concentric and eccentric contractions.

— Have players perform three sets of 12 to 15 repetitions to train strength and endurance in the working muscles.

— Set rest periods between sets of exercise that is specific to the sport of tennis, generally between 20 and 30 seconds.

— Do not strength train immediately before skill-oriented practice or tennis play.

— Hold strength-training sessions after tennis or on days when tennis play is lighter or tennis is not played at all.

— Do not recommend maximal lifts, due to the risk of injury.

Adaptations to Strength Training

Two primary phases or adaptations occur in the body in

response to strength training. These responses are termed neurological and morphological.

The neurological response occurs as the body's nerves become more organized and better at communicating with the working muscles during a particular exercise or movement pattern. This response can occur quite rapidly and is usually the reason that players may say that they feel stronger in as little as two weeks after starting a strength-training program. This adaptation is very important, as the body is dependent on proper recruitment or communication between the nerves and the working muscles during all activities.

The morphological or structural adaptation involves actual change or adaptation within the muscles being exercised or trained. This adaptation is thought to involve both the enlargement of the existing muscle fibers that comprise a muscle and the splitting and development of new or more muscle fibers within a muscle. Scientists are still unsure of the exact amount and extent of each of these two adaptations; however, structural changes do occur within the muscle. This change takes at least six to eight weeks, however, and so people must adhere to a strength-training program for an extended period to see this result.

Setting the Resistance Level for Strength Training

One of the most difficult concepts for both players and coaches to understand is how to determine the amount of weight appropriate for strength training. One widespread recommendation is to apply the repetition maximum (RM) concept. This concept allows a player or coach to set the proper resistance level based on the goal of the exercise. In tennis, as stated previously, 12 to 15 reps per set are often used to promote muscular endurance and strength. Therefore, using the RM concept, a player or coach can select a weight at which the player can perform 12 repetitions (12RM) or 15 repetitions (15RM) continuously, without breaking form, and at the conclusion of which the working muscles are fatigued.

To illustrate this concept, let us examine an example of a player doing a bicep curl with a free weight. If the player chooses an 85-pound weight, he or she may be able to do only one rep or may not even be able to lift the weight off the rack! This weight would not allow the player to perform 12 or 15 reps. Likewise, if the player chose a 2-pound weight, he or she could perform 12 to 15 reps and feel no fatigue afterward. Therefore, carefully selecting a resistance level somewhere between these two extremes would result in the player's finding the optimum resistance level for the RM level being performed. In general, for a sport like tennis, it is safer to fatigue a muscle with repetitions than with excessive weight. Most players use too much weight to impress coaches and other players, and this practice can lead to early fatigue or even injury.

Overload and Progression

There are two final important concepts in physiology: overload and progression. These concepts apply to any type of training program. The concept of overload is that an exercise or activity must provide some type of overload to the system in order to improve the system's function in terms of strength, endurance, speed, agility, or other qualities. For example, appropriate means for overloading in strength training might be free weights, tubing, weight machines, or one's own body weight.

Here is an example of applying overload to a program. A player initially is given an alley hop-type exercise to improve lateral movement and lower extremity strength. However, after the player does the alley hop exercise in different formats for several workouts, she or he will need more resistance in order to overload the system. The coach can place a stretch cord or tubing around the player's waist to resist the movement in each direction, forcing the player's musculature to work against a greater resistance or overload.

The concept of progression is also critically important when designing any type of training program for tennis players. This concept states that any program must be continually progressed to allow the player to develop and improve beyond the initial improvements. Program progression includes increasing the duration, frequency, or intensity of the program being performed. Without progression, a resistance-training program becomes boring and does not continue to stimulate the muscles to develop additional strength or endurance. Both the amount of resistance and the number of repetitions can be increased to provide progression to a program.

12

ITF-Rules of Tennis

1. The Court (Old 1 & 34)

The court shall be a rectangle, 78 feet (23.77 m) long and, for singles matches, 27 feet (8.23 m) wide. For doubles matches, the court shall be 36 feet (10.97 m) wide.

The court shall be divided across the middle by a net suspended by a cord or metal cable which shall pass over or be attached to two net posts at a height of 31.2 feet (1.07 m). The net shall be fully extended so that it completely fills the space between the two net posts and it must be of sufficiently small mesh to ensure that a ball cannot pass through it. The height of the net shall be 3 feet (0.914 m) at the centre, where it shall be held down tightly by a strap. A band shall cover the cord or metal cable and the top of the net. The strap and band shall be completely white.

— The maximum diameter of the cord or metal cable shall be 1.3 inch (0.8 cm).

— The maximum width of the strap shall be 2 inches (5 cm).

— The band shall be between 2 inches (5 cm) and 21.2 inches (6.35 cm) deep on each side.

For doubles matches, the centres of the net posts shall be 3 feet (0.914 m) outside the doubles court on each side.

For singles matches, if a singles net is used, the centres of the net posts shall be 3 feet (0.914 m) outside the singles court on each side. If a doubles net is used, then the net shall be supported, at a height of 31.2 feet (1.07 m), by two singles sticks, the centres of which shall be 3 feet (0.914 m) outside the singles court on each side.

— The net posts shall not be more than 6 inches (15 cm) square or 6 inches (15 cm) in diameter.

— The singles sticks shall not be more than 3 inches (7.5 cm) square or 3 inches (7.5 cm) in diameter.

— The net posts and singles sticks shall not be more than 1 inch (2.5 cm) above the top of the net cord.

The lines at the ends of the court are called baselines and the lines at the sides of the court are called sidelines.

Two lines shall be drawn between the singles sidelines, 21 feet (6.40 m) from each side of the net, parallel with the net. These lines are called the servicelines. On each side of the net, the area between the serviceline and the net shall be divided into two equal parts, the service courts, by the centre serviceline. The centre serviceline shall be drawn parallel with the singles sidelines and half way between them.

Each baseline shall be divided in half by a centre mark, 4 inches (10 cm) in length, which shall be drawn inside the court and parallel with the singles sidelines.

— The centre service line and centre mark shall be 2 inches (5 cm) wide.

— The other lines of the court shall be between 1 inch (2.5 cm) and 2 inches (5 cm) wide, except that the base lines may be up to 4 inches (10 cm) wide.

All court measurements shall be made to the outside of the lines and all lines of the court shall be of the same colour clearly contrasting with the colour of the surface.

No advertising is allowed on the court, net, strap, band, net posts or singles sticks except as provided in Appendix III.

2. Permanent Fixtures (Old 2)

The permanent fixtures of the court include the backstops and sidestops, the spectators, the stands and seats for spectators, all other fixtures around and above the court, the chair umpire, line umpires, net umpire and ball persons when in their recognised positions.

In a singles match played with a doubles net and singles sticks, the net posts and the part of the net outside the singles sticks are permanent fixtures and are not considered as net posts or part of the net.

3. The Ball (Old 3, 13, 27 & 32)

Balls, which are approved for play under the Rules of Tennis, must comply with the specifications in Appendix I.

The International Tennis Federation shall rule on the question of whether any ball or prototype complies with Appendix I or is otherwise approved, or not approved, for play. Such ruling may be taken on its own initiative, or upon application by any party with a bona fide interest therein, including any player, equipment manufacturer or National Association or members thereof. Such rulings and applications shall be made in accordance with the applicable Review and Hearing Procedures of the International Tennis Federation (see Appendix VI).

The event organisers must announce in advance of the event:

a. The number of balls for play (2, 3, 4 or 6).

b. The ball change policy, if any.

Ball changes, if any, can be made either:

i. After an agreed odd number of games, in which case, the first ball change in the match shall take place two games earlier than for the rest of the match, to make allowance for the warm-up. A tie-break game counts as one game for the ball change. A ball change shall not take place at the beginning of a tie-break game. In this case, the ball change shall be delayed until the beginning of the second game of the next set; or

ii. At the beginning of a set

If a ball gets broken during play, the point shall be replayed.

Case 1: If a ball is soft at the end of a point, should the point be replayed?

Decision: If the ball is soft, not broken, the point shall not be replayed. Note: Any ball to be used in a tournament which is played under the Rules of Tennis, must be named on the official ITF list of approved balls issued by the International Tennis Federation.

4. The Racket (Old 4)

Rackets, which are approved for play under the Rules of Tennis, must comply with the specifications in Appendix II.

The International Tennis Federation shall rule on the question of whether any racket or prototype complies with Appendix II or is otherwise approved, or not approved, for play. Such ruling may be undertaken on its own initiative, or upon application by any party with a bona fide interest therein, including any player, equipment manufacturer or National Association or members thereof. Such rulings and applications shall be made in accordance with the applicable Review and

Hearing Procedures of the International Tennis Federation (see Appendix VI).

Case 1: Is more than one set of strings allowed on the hitting surface of a racket?

Decision: No. The rule mentions a pattern (not patterns) of crossed strings. (See Appendix II)

Case 2: Is the stringing pattern of a racket considered to be generally uniform and flat if the strings are on more than one plane?

Decision: No.

Case 3: Can vibration damping devices be placed on the strings of a racket?

If so, where can they be placed?

Decision: Yes, but these devices may only be placed outside the pattern of the crossed strings.

Case 4: During a point, a player accidentally breaks the strings. Can the player continue to play another point with this racket? Decision: Yes, except where specifically prohibited by event organisers. Case 5: Is a player allowed to use more than one racket at any time during play?

Decision: No.

Case 6: Can a battery that affects playing characteristics be incorporated into a racket?

Decision: No. A battery is prohibited because it is an energy source, as are solar cells and other similar devices.

5. Score in a Game (Old 26 & 27)

a. Standard game

A standard game is scored as follows with the server's score being called first:

No point - "Love"
First point - "15"
Second point - "30"
Third point - "40"
Fourth point - "Game"

except that if each player/team has won three points, the score is "Deuce". After "Deuce", the score is "Advantage" for the player/team who wins the next point. If that same player/team also wins the next point, that player/team wins the "Game"; if the opposing player/team wins the next point, the score is again "Deuce". A player/team needs to win two consecutive points immediately after "Deuce" to win the "Game".

b. Tie-break game

During a tie-break game, points are scored "Zero","1", "2", "3", etc. The first player/team to win seven points wins the "Game" and "Set", provided there is a margin of two points over the opponent(s). If necessary, the tie-break game shall continue until this margin is achieved. The player whose turn it is to serve shall serve the first point of the tie-break game. The following two points shall be served by the opponent(s) (in doubles, the player of the opposing team due to serve next). After this, each player/team shall serve alternately for two consecutive points until the end of the tie-break game (in doubles, the rotation of service within each team shall continue in the same order as during that set).

The player/team whose turn it was to serve first in the tie-break game shall be the receiver in the first game of the following set. Additional approved alternative scoring methods can be found in Appendix IV.

6. Score in a Set (Old 27)

There are different methods of scoring in a set. The two

main methods are the "Advantage Set" and the "Tie-break Set". Either method may be used provided that the one to be used is announced in advance of the event. If the "Tie-break Set" method is to be used, it must also be announced whether the final set will be played as a "Tie-break Set" or an "Advantage Set".

a. "Advantage Set"

The first player/team to win six games wins that "Set", provided there is a margin of two games over the opponent(s). If necessary, the set shall continue until this margin is achieved.

b. "Tie-break Set"

The first player/team to win six games wins that "Set", provided there is a margin of two games over the opponent(s). If the score reaches six games all, a tie-break game shall be played.

Additional approved alternative scoring methods can be found in Appendix IV.

7. Score in a Match (Old 28)

A match can be played to the best of 3 sets (a player/team needs to win 2 sets to win the match) or to the best of 5 sets (a player/team needs to win 3 sets to win the match).

Additional approved alternative scoring methods can be found in Appendix IV.

8. Server and Receiver (Old 5)

The players/teams shall stand on opposite sides of the net. The server is the player who puts the ball into play for the first point. The receiver is the player who is ready to return the ball served by the server.

Case 1: Is the receiver allowed to stand outside the lines of the court?

Decision: Yes. The receiver may take any position inside or outside the lines on the receiver's side of the net.

9. Choice of Ends and Service (Old 6)

The choice of ends and the choice to be server or receiver in the first game shall be decided by toss before the warm-up starts. The player/team who wins the toss may choose:

a. To be server or receiver in the first game of the match, in which case the opponent(s) shall choose the end of the court for the first game of the match; or

b. The end of the court for the first game of the match, in which case the opponent(s) shall choose to be server or receiver for the first game of the match; or

c. To require the opponent(s) to make one of the above choices

Case 1: Do both players/teams have the right to new choices if the warm-up is stopped and the players leave the court?

Decision: Yes. The result of the original toss stands, but new choices may be made by both players/teams.

10. Change of Ends (Old 16 & 27)

The players shall change ends at the end of the first, third and every subsequent odd game of each set. The players shall also change ends at the end of each set unless the total number of games in that set is even, in which case the players change ends at the end of the first game of the next set. During a tie-break game, players shall change ends after every six points.

11. Ball in Play (Old 17)

Unless a fault or a let is called, the ball is in play from the moment the server hits the ball, and remains in play until the point is decided.

12. Ball Touches a Line (Old 22)

If a ball touches a line, it is regarded as touching the court bounded by that line.

13. Ball Touches a Permanent Fixture (Old 23)

If the ball in play touches a permanent fixture after it has hit the correct court, the player who hit the ball wins the point. If the ball in play touches a permanent fixture before it hits the ground, the player who hit the ball loses the point.

14. Order of Service (Old 15 & 35)

At the end of each standard game, the receiver shall become the server and the server shall become the receiver for the next game. In doubles, the team due to serve in the first game of each set shall decide which player shall serve for that game. Similarly, before the second game starts, their opponents shall decide which player shall serve for that game. The partner of the player who served in the first game shall serve in the third game and the partner of the player who served in the second game shall serve in the fourth game. This rotation shall continue until the end of the set.

15. Order of Receiving in Doubles (Old 35, 36 & 40)

The team which is due to receive in the first game of a set shall decide which player shall receive the first point in the game. Similarly, before the second game starts, their opponents shall decide which player shall receive the first point of that game. The player who was the receiver's partner for the first point of the game shall receive the second point and this rotation shall continue until the end of the game and the set.

After the receiver has returned the ball, either player in a team can hit the ball.

Case 1: Is one member of a doubles team allowed to play alone against the opponents?

Decision: No.

16. The Service (Old 7)

Immediately before starting the service motion, the server shall stand at rest with both feet behind (i.e. further from the net than) the baseline and within the imaginary extensions of the centre mark and the sideline. The server shall then release the ball by hand in any direction and hit the ball with the racket before the ball hits the ground. The service motion is completed at the moment that the player's racket hits or misses the ball. A player who is able to use only one arm may use the racket for the release of the ball.

17. Serving (Old 9 & 27)

When serving in a standard game, the server shall stand behind alternate halves of the court, starting from the right half of the court in every game. In a tie-break game, the serve shall be served from behind alternate halves of the court, with the first served from the right half of the court. The serve shall pass over the net and hit the service court diagonally opposite, before the receiver returns it.

18. Foot Fault (Old 7 & 8)

During the service motion, the server shall not:

a. Change position by walking or running, although slight movements of the feet are permitted; or

b. Touch the baseline or the court with either foot; or

c. Touch the area outside the imaginary extension of the sideline with either foot; or

d. Touch the imaginary extension of the centre mark with either foot.

If the server breaks this rule it is a "Foot Fault".

Case 1: In a singles match, is the server allowed to serve standing behind the part of the baseline between the singles sideline and the doubles sideline?

Decision: No.

Case 2: Is the server allowed to have one or both feet off the ground?

Decision: Yes.

19. Service Fault (Old 10 & 39)

The service is a fault if:

a. The server breaks rules 16, 17, or 18; or

b. The server misses the ball when trying to hit it; or

c. The ball served touches a permanent fixture, singles stick or net post before it hits the ground; or

d. The ball served touches the server or server's partner, or anything the server or server's partner is wearing or carrying.

Case 1: After tossing a ball to serve, the server decides not to hit it and catches it instead. Is this a fault?

Decision: No. A player, who tosses the ball and then decides not to hit it, is allowed to catch the ball with the hand or the racket, or to let the ball bounce.

Case 2: During a singles match played on a court with net posts and singles sticks, the ball served hits a singles stick and then hits the correct service court. Is this a fault?

Decision: Yes.

20. Second Service (Old 11)

If the first service is a fault, the server shall serve again without delay from behind the same half of the court from which that fault was served, unless the service was from the wrong half.

21. When to Serve and Receive (Old 12 & 30)

The server shall not serve until the receiver is ready. However, the receiver shall play to the reasonable pace of the server and shall be ready to receive within a reasonable time of the server being ready. A receiver who attempts to return the service shall be considered as being ready. If it is demonstrated that the receiver is not ready, the service cannot be called a fault.

22. The Let During a Serve (Old 14)

The serve is a let if:

a. The ball served touches the net, strap or band, and is otherwise good; or, after touching the net, strap or band, touches the receiver or the receiver's partner or anything they wear or carry before hitting the ground; or

b. The ball is served when the receiver is not ready.

In the case of a service let, that particular service shall not count, and the server shall serve again, but a service let does not cancel a previous fault.

23. The Let (Old 13 & 25)

In all cases when a let is called, except when a service let is called on a second service, the whole point shall be replayed.

Case 1: When the ball is in play, another ball rolls onto court. A let is called. The server had previously served a fault. Is the server now entitled to a first service or second service?

Decision: First service. The whole point must be replayed.

24. Player Loses Point (Old 18, 19, 20 & 40)

The point is lost if:

a. The player serves two consecutive faults; or

b. The player does not return the ball in play before it bounces twice consecutively; or

c. The player returns the ball in play so that it hits the ground, or an object, outside the correct court; or

d. The player returns the ball in play so that, before it bounces, it hits a permanent fixture; or

e. The player deliberately carries or catches the ball in play on the racket or deliberately touches it with the racket more than once; or

f. The player or the racket, whether in the player's hand or not, or anything which the player is wearing or carrying touches the net, net posts/singles sticks, cord or metal cable, strap or band, or the opponent's court at any time while the ball is in play; or

g. The player hits the ball before it has passed the net; or

h. The ball in play touches the player or anything that the player is wearing or carrying, except the racket; or

i. The ball in play touches the racket when the player is not holding it; or

j. The player deliberately and materially changes the shape of the racket when the ball is in play; or

k. In doubles, both players touch the ball when returning it.

Case 1: After the server has served a first service, the racket falls out of the server's hand and touches the net before the ball has bounced. Is this a service fault, or does the server lose the point?

Decision: The server loses the point because the racket touches the net while the ball is in play.

Case 2: After the server has served a first service, the racket falls out of the server's hand and touches the net after the ball has bounced outside the correct court. Is this a service fault, or does the server lose the point? Decision. This is a service fault because when the racket touched the net the ball was no longer in play.

Case 3. In a doubles match, the receiver's partner touches the net before the ball that has been served touches the ground outside the correct service court. What is the correct decision?

Decision. The receiving team loses the point because the receiver's partner touched the net while the ball was in play.

Case 4: Does a player lose the point if an imaginary line in the extension of the net is crossed before or after hitting the ball? Decision: The player does not lose the point in either case provided the player does not touch the opponent's court.

Case 5. Is a player allowed to jump over the net into the opponent's court while the ball is in play?

Decision. No. The player loses the point.

Case 6. A player throws the racket at the ball in play. Both the racket and the ball land in the court on the

opponent's side of the net and the opponent(s) is unable to reach the ball. Which player wins the point? Decision. The player who threw the racket at the ball loses the point.

Case 7. A ball that has just been served hits the receiver or in doubles the receiver's partner before it touches the ground. Which player wins the point? Decision. The server wins the point, unless it is a service let.

Case 8. A player standing outside the court hits the ball or catches it before it bounces and claims the point because the ball was definitely going out of the correct court.

Decision. The player loses the point, unless it is a good return, in which case the point continues.

25. A Good Return (Old 24)

It is a good return if:

a. The ball touches the net, net posts/singles sticks, cord or metal cable, strap or band, provided that it passes over any of them and hits the ground within the correct court; except as provided in Rule 2 and 24 (d); or

b. After the ball in play has hit the ground within the correct court and has spun or been blown back over the net, the player reaches over the net and plays the ball into the correct court, provided that the player does not break Rule 24; or

c. The ball is returned outside the net posts, either above or below the level of the top of the net, even though it touches the net posts, provided that it hits the ground in the correct court; except as provided in Rules 2 and 24 (d); or

d. The ball passes under the net cord between the singles stick and the adjacent net post without touching either net, net cord or net post and hits the ground in the correct court, or

e. The player's racket passes over the net after hitting the ball on the player's own side of the net and the ball hits the ground in the correct court; or

f. The player hits the ball in play, which hits another ball lying in the correct court.

Case 1: A player returns a ball which then hits a singles stick and hits the ground in the correct court. Is this is a good return? Decision: Yes. However, if the ball is served and hits the singles stick, it is a service fault.

Case 2: A ball in play hits another ball which is lying in the correct court.

What is the correct decision?

Decision: Play continues. However, if it is not clear that the actual ball in play has been returned, a let should be called.

26. HINDRANCE (OLD 21,25 & 36)

If a player is hindered in playing the point by a deliberate act of the opponent(s), the player shall win the point.

However, the point shall be replayed if a player is hindered in playing the point by either an unintentional act of the opponent(s), or something outside the player's own control (not including a permanent fixture). Case 1: Is an unintentional double hit a hindrance?

Decision: No. See also Rule 24 (e).

Case 2: A player claims to have stopped play because the player thought that the opponent(s) was being hindered. Is this a hindrance? Decision: No, the player loses the point.

Case 3: A ball in play hits a bird flying over the court. Is this a hindrance?

Decision: Yes, the point shall be replayed.

Case 4: During a point, a ball or other object that was lying on the player's side of the net when the point started hinders the player. Is this a hindrance?

Decision: No.

Case 5: In doubles, where are the server's partner and receiver's partner allowed to stand?

Decision: The server's partner and the receiver's partner may take any position on their own side of the net, inside or outside the court. However, if a player is creating a hindrance to the opponent(s), the hindrance rule should be used.

27. Correcting Errors (New)

As a principle, when an error in respect of the Rules of Tennis is discovered, all points previously played shall stand. Errors so discovered shall be corrected as follows:

a. (Old 9a, 11, & 27b.iii)

During a standard game or a tie-break game, if a player serves from the wrong half of the court, this should be corrected as soon as the error is discovered and the server shall serve from the correct half of the court according to the score. A fault that was served before the error was discovered shall stand.

b. (Old 16)

During a standard game or a tie-break game, if the players are at the wrong ends of the court, the error should be corrected as soon as it is discovered and the server shall serve from the correct end of the court according to the score.

c. (Old 15 & 37)

If a player serves out of turn during a standard game, the player who was originally due to serve shall serve as soon as the error is discovered. However, if a game is completed before the error is discovered the order of service shall remain as altered.

A fault that was served by the opponents(s) before the error was discovered shall not stand.

In doubles, if the partners of one team serve out of turn, a fault that was served before the error was discovered shall stand.

d. (Old 27, Case 3)

If a player serves out of turn during a tie-break game and the error is discovered after an even number of points have been played, the error is corrected immediately. If the error is discovered after an odd number of points have been played, the order of service shall remain as altered. A fault that was served by the opponent(s) before the error was discovered shall not stand.

In doubles, if the partners of one team serve out of turn, a fault that was served before the error was discovered shall stand.

e. (Old 38)

During a standard game or a tie-break game in doubles, if there is an error in the order of receiving, this shall remain as altered until the end of the game in which the error is discovered. For the next game in which they are the receivers in that set, the partners shall then resume the original order of receiving.

f. (Old 27, Case 1)

If in error a tie-break game is started at 6 games all, when it was previously agreed that the set would be an "Advantage set", the error shall be corrected immediately if only one point has been played. If the error is discovered after the second point is in play, the set will continue as a "Tie-break set".

g. (Old 27, Case 2)

If in error a standard game is started at 6 games all, when it was previously agreed that the set would be a "Tie-break set", the error shall be corrected immediately if only one point has been played. If the error is discovered after the second point is in play, the set will continue as an "Advantage set" until the score reaches 8 games all (or a higher even number), when a tie-break game shall be played.

h. (New)

If in error an "Advantage set" or "Tie-break set" is started, when it was previously agreed that the final set would be a deciding match tie-break, the error shall be corrected immediately if only one point has been played. If the error is discovered after the second point is in play, the set will continue either until a player or team wins three games (and therefore the set) or until the score reaches 2 games all, when a deciding match tie-break shall be played. However, if the error is discovered after the fifth game has started, the set will continue as a "Tie-break set" (See Appendix IV).

i. (Old 32)

If the balls are not changed in the correct sequence, the error shall be corrected when the player/team who should have served with new balls is next due to serve a new game. Thereafter the balls shall be changed so that the number of games between ball changes shall be that originally agreed. Balls should not be changed during a game.

28. Role of Court Officials (Old 29)

For matches where officials are appointed, their roles and responsibilities can be found in Appendix V.

29. Continous Play (Old 29 & 30)

As a principle, play should be continuous, from the time the match starts (when the first service of the match is put in play) until the match finishes.

a. Between points, a maximum of twenty (20) seconds is allowed.

   When the players change ends at the end of a game, a maximum of ninety (90) seconds are allowed. However, after the first game of each set and during a tie-break game, play shall be continuous and the players shall change ends without a rest.

   At the end of each set there shall be a set break of a maximum of one hundred and twenty (120) seconds.

   The maximum time starts from the moment that one point finishes until the first service is struck for the next point.

   Organisers of professional circuits may apply for ITF approval to extend the ninety (90) seconds allowed when the players change ends at the end of a game and the one hundred and twenty (120) seconds allowed at a set break.

b. If, for reasons outside the player's control, clothing, footwear or necessary equipment (excluding the racket) is broken or needs to be replaced, the player may be allowed reasonable extra time to rectify the problem.

c. No extra time shall be given to allow a player to recover condition.

However, a player suffering from a treatable medical condition may be allowed one medical time-out of three minutes for the treatment of that medical condition. A limited number of toilet/change of attire breaks may also be allowed, if this is announced in advance of the event.

d. Event organisers may allow a rest period of a maximum of ten (10) minutes if this is announced in advance of the event. This rest period can be taken after the 3rd set in a best of 5 sets match, or after the 2nd set in a best of 3 sets match.

e. The warm-up time shall be a maximum of five (5) minutes, unless otherwise decided by the event organisers.

30. Coaching (Old 31)

Coaching is considered to be communication, advice or instruction of any kind, audible or visible, to a player.

In team events where there is a team captain sitting on-court, the team captain may coach the player(s) during a set break and when the players change ends at the end of a game, but not when the players change ends after the first game of each set and not during a tie-break game. In all other matches, coaching is not allowed.

Case 1: Is a player allowed to be coached, if the coaching is given by signals in a discreet way?

Decision: No.

Case 2: Is a player allowed to receive coaching when play is suspended?

Decision: Yes.

Rules of Wheelchair Tennis

The game of wheelchair tennis follows the ITF Rules of Tennis with the following exceptions.

a. The Two Bounce Rule

The wheelchair tennis player is allowed two bounces of the ball. The player must return the ball before it hits the ground a third time. The second bounce can be either in or out of the court boundaries.

b. The Wheelchair

The wheelchair is considered part of the body and all applicable rules, which apply to a player's body, shall apply to the wheelchair.

c. The Service

i. The service shall be delivered in the following manner. Immediately before commencing the service, the server shall be in a stationary position. The server shall then be allowed one push before striking the ball.

ii. The server shall throughout the delivery of the service not touch with any wheel, any area other than that behind the baseline within the imaginary extension of the centre mark and sideline.

iii. If conventional methods for the service are physically impossible for a quadriplegic player, then the player or an individual may drop the ball for such a player. However, the same method of serving must be used each time.

d. Player Loses Point A player loses a point if:

i. The player fails to return the ball before it has touched the ground three times; or

ii. Subject to rule e) below the player uses any part of his feet or lower extremities as brakes or as stabilisers while delivering service, stroking a ball, turning or stopping against the ground or against any wheel while the ball is in play; or

iii. The player fails to keep one buttock in contact with his wheelchair seat when contacting the ball.

e. Propelling the Chair with the Foot

i. If due to lack of capacity a player is unable to propel the wheelchair via the wheel then he may propel the wheelchair using one foot.

ii. Even if in accordance with rule e) i. above a player is permitted to propel the chair using one foot, no part of the player's foot may be in contact with the ground:

  a) during the forward motion of the swing, including when the racket strikes the ball;

  b) from the initiation of the service motion until the racket strikes the ball.

iii. A player in breach of this rule shall lose the point.

f. Wheelchair/Able-bodied Tennis

Where a wheelchair tennis player is playing with or against an ablebodied person in singles or doubles, the Rules of Wheelchair Tennis shall apply for the wheelchair player while the Rules of Tennis for ablebodied tennis shall apply for the able-bodied player. In this instance, the wheelchair player is allowed two bounces while the able-bodied player is allowed only one bounce.

Note: The definition of lower extremities is: -the lower limb, including the buttocks, hip, thigh, leg, ankle and foot.

Amendment to the Rules of Tennis

The official and decisive text to the Rules of Tennis shall be for ever in the English language and no alteration or interpretation of such Rules shall be made except at an Annual General Meeting of the Council, nor unless notice of the resolution embodying such alteration shall have been received by the Federation in accordance with Article 17 of the Constitution of ITF Ltd Notice of Resolutions) and such resolution or one having the like effect shall be carried by a majority of two-thirds of the votes recorded in respect of the same.

Any alteration so made shall take effect as from the first day of January following unless the Meeting shall by the like majority decide otherwise. The Board of Directors shall have power, however, to settle all urgent questions of interpretation subject to confirmation at the General Meeting next following.

This Rule shall not be altered at any time without the unanimous consent of a General Meeting of the Council.

Appendix I
The Ball

a. The ball shall have a uniform outer surface consisting of a fabric cover and shall be white or yellow in colour. If there are any seams they shall be stitchless.

b. The ball shall conform to these requirements and have a weight (mass) of more than 1.975 ounces (56.0 grams) and less than 2.095 ounces (59.4 grams).

c. More than one type of ball is specified. Each ball shall have a bound of more than 53 inches (134.62 cm) and less than 58 inches (147.32 cm) when dropped 100 inches (254.00 cm) upon a flat, rigid surface e.g. concrete. Ball Type 1 (fast speed) shall have a forward deformation of more than .195 inches (.495 cm) and less than .235 inches (.597 cm) and return deformation of more than .265 inches (.673 cm) and less than .360 inches (.914 cm) at 18 lb (8.165 kg) load. Ball Types 2 (medium speed) and 3 (slow speed) shall have a forward deformation of more than .220 inches (.559 cm) and less than .290 inches (.737 cm) and return deformation of more than .315 inches (.800 cm) and less than .425 inches (1.080 cm) at 18 lb (8.165 kg) load. The two deformation figures shall be the averages of three individual readings along three axes of the ball and no two individual readings shall differ by more than .030 inches (.076 cm) in each case.

d. For play above 4,000 feet (1219 m) in altitude above sea level, two additional types of ball may be used.

   i. The first type is identical to Ball Type 2 (medium speed) as defined above except that the ball shall have a bound of more than 48 inches (121.92 cm) and less than 53 inches (134.62 cm) and shall have an internal pressure that is greater than the external pressure. This type of tennis ball is commonly known as a pressurised ball.

   ii. The second type is identical to Ball Type 2 (medium speed) as defined above except that the ball shall have an internal pressure that is approximately equal to the external pressure and have been acclimatised for 60 days or more at the altitude of the specific tournament. This type of tennis ball is commonly known as a zero-pressure or non-pressurised ball.

   iii. The third type of ball which is recommended for use for play on any court surface type above 4,000 feet (1219 m) in altitude is the Ball Type 3 (slow speed), as defined above.

e. All tests for bound, size and deformation shall be made in accordance with the regulations below.

Case 1: Which ball type should be used on which court surface?

Decision: 3 different types of balls are approved for play under the Rules Tennis, however:

a. Ball Type 1 (fast speed) is intended for play on slow pace court surfaces

b. Ball Type 2 (medium speed) is intended for play on medium/medium-fast pace court surfaces

c. Ball Type 3 (slow speed) is intended for play on fast pace court surfaces

Regulations for Making Tests

i. Unless otherwise specified all tests shall be made at a temperature of approximately 68° Fahrenheit (20° Celsius) and a relative humidity of approximately 60%. All balls shall be removed from their container and kept at the recognised temperature and humidity for 24 hours prior to testing, and shall be at that temperature and humidity when the test is commenced.

ii. Unless otherwise specified the limits are for a test conducted in an atmospheric pressure resulting in a barometric reading of approximately 30 inches (76 cm).

iii. Other standards may be fixed for localities where the average tem-perature, humidity or average barometric pressure at which the game is being played differ materially from 68° Fahrenheit (20° Celsius), 60% and 30 inches (76 cm) respectively. Applications for such adjusted standards may be made by any National Association to the

International Tennis Federation and, if approved, shall be adopted for such localities.

iv. In all tests for diameter, a ring gauge shall be used consisting of a metal plate, preferably non-corrosive, of a uniform thickness of oneeighth of an inch (.318 cm). In the case of Ball Type 1 (fast speed) and Ball Type 2 (medium speed) balls there shall be two circular openings in the plate measuring 2.575 inches (6.541 cm) and 2.700 inches (6.858 cm) in diameter respectively. In the case of Ball Type 3 (slow speed) balls there shall be two circular openings in the plate measuring 2.750 inches (6.985 cm) and 2.875 inches (7.302 cm) in diameter respectively. The inner surface of the gauge shall have a convex profile with a radius of one-sixteenth of an inch (.159 cm). The ball shall not drop through the smaller opening by its own weight and shall drop through the larger opening by its own weight.

v. In all tests for deformation conducted under Rule 3, the machine designed by Percy Herbert Stevens and patented in Great Britain under Patent No. 230250, together with the subsequent additions and improvements thereto, including the modifications required to take return deformations, shall be employed. Other machines may be specified which give equivalent readings to the Stevens machine and these may be used for testing ball deformation where such machines have been given approval by the International Tennis Federation.

vi. The procedure for carrying out tests is as follows and should take place in the order specified:

   a. Pre-compression-before any ball is tested it shall be steadily compressed by approximately one inch (2.54 cm) on each of three diameters at right angles to one another in succession; this process to be carried out three times (nine compressions in all). All tests are to be completed within two hours of pre-compression.

b. Weight (mass) test (as above).

c. Size test (as in paragraph iv above).

d. Deformation test-the ball is placed in position on the modified Stevens machine so that neither platen of the machine is in contact with the cover seam. The contact weight is applied, the pointer and the mark brought level, and the dials set to zero. The test weight is placed on the beam in a position that is equivalent to a load of 18 lb (8.165 kg) on the ball, after which the wheel is turned at a uniform speed such that five seconds elapse from the instant the beam leaves its seat until the pointer is brought level with the mark. When turning ceases the reading is recorded (forward deformation). The wheel is turned again until figure ten is reached on the scale (1 inch (2.54 cm) deformation). The wheel is then rotated in the opposite direction at a uniform speed (thus releasing pressure) until the beam pointer again coincides with the mark. After waiting ten seconds, the pointer is adjusted to the mark if necessary. The reading is then recorded (return deformation). This procedure is repeated on each ball across the two diameters at right angles to the initial position and to each other.

e. Bound test (as above)-measurements are to be taken from the concrete base to the bottom of the ball.

Classification of Court Surface Pace

The ITF test method used for determining the pace of a

court surface is test method ITF CS 01/01 (ITF Surface Pace Rating) as described in the ITF publication entitled "An initial ITF study on performance standards for tennis court surfaces".

Court surfaces which are found to have an ITF Surface Pace Rating of between 0 and 35 shall be classified as being Category 1 (slow pace). Examples of court surface types which conform to this classification will include most clay courts and other types of unbound mineral surface. Court surfaces which are found to have an ITF Surface Pace Rating of between 30 and 45 shall be classified as being Category 2 (medium/mediumfast pace). Examples of court surface types which conform to this classification will include most hardcourts with various acrylic type coatings plus some textile surfaces.

Court surfaces which are found to have an ITF Surface Pace Rating of over 40 shall be classified as being Category 3 (fast pace). Examples of court surface types which conform to this classification will include most natural grass, artificial turf and some textile surfaces.

Note: The proposed overlap in ITF Surface Pace Rating values for the above categories is to allow some latitude in ball selection.

Appendix II
The Racket

a. The hitting surface of the racket shall be flat and consist of a pattern of crossed strings connected to a frame and alternately interlaced or bonded where they cross. The stringing pattern must be generally uniform and, in particular, not less dense in the centre than in any other area. The racket shall be designed and strung such that the playing characteristics are identical on both faces. The strings shall be free of attached objects and protrusions other than those utilised solely and specifically to limit or prevent wear and tear or vibration. These objects and protrusions must be reasonable in size and placement for such purposes.

b. The frame of the racket shall not exceed 29 inches (73.66 cm) in overall length, including the handle. The frame of the racket shall not exceed 121.2 inches (31.75 cm) in overall width. The hitting surface shall not exceed 151.2 inches (39.37 cm) in overall length, and 111.2 inches (29.21 cm) in overall width.

c. The frame, including the handle, shall be free of attached objects and devices other than those utilised solely and specifically to limit or prevent wear and tear or vibration, or to distribute weight. Any objects and devices must be reasonable in size and placement for such purposes.

d. The frame, including the handle, and the strings, shall be free of any device which makes it possible to change materially the shape of the racket, or to change the weight distribution in the direction of the longitudinal axis of the racket which would alter the swing moment of inertia, or to deliberately change any physical property which may affect the performance of the racket during the playing of a point. No energy source that in any way changes or affects the playing characteristics of a racket may be built into or attached to a racket.

Appendix III
Advertsing

1. Advertising is permitted on the net as long as it is placed on the part of the net that is within 3 feet (0.914 m) from the centre of the net posts and is produced in such a way that it does not interfere

with the vision of the players or the playing conditions.

2. Advertising and other marks or material placed at the back and sides of the court shall be permitted unless it interferes with the vision of the players or the playing conditions.
3. Advertising and other marks or material placed on the court surface outside the lines is permitted unless it interferes with the vision of the players or the playing conditions.
4. Notwithstanding paragraphs (1), (2) and (3) above, any advertising, marks or material placed on the net or placed at the back and sides of the court, or on the court surface outside the lines may not contain white or yellow or other light colours that may interfere with the vision of the players or the playing conditions.
5. Advertising and other marks or material are not permitted on the court surface inside the lines of the court.

APPENDIX IV
ALTERNATIVE SCORING METHODS

Score in a Game:

"No-Ad" Scoring Method

This alternative scoring method may be used.

A standard game is scored as follows with the server's score being called first:

No point	- "Love"
First point	- "15"
Second point	- "30"

Third point - "40"

Fourth point - "Game"

If both players/teams have won three points each, the score is "Deuce" and a deciding point shall be played. The receiver(s) shall choose whether to receive the service from the right half or the left half of the court. In doubles, the players of the receiving team cannot change positions to receive this deciding point. The player/team who wins the deciding point wins the "Game". In mixed doubles, the player of the same gender as the server shall receive the deciding point. The players of the receiving team cannot change positions to receive the deciding point.

Score in a Set:

1. "Short" Sets

The first player/team who wins four games wins that set, provided there is a margin of two games over the opponent(s). If the score reaches four games all, a tie-break game shall be played.

2. Deciding Match Tie-break (7 Points)

When the score in a match is one set all, or two sets all in best of five sets matches, one tie-break game shall be played to decide the match. This tie-break game replaces the deciding final set.

The player/team who first wins seven points shall win this match tie-break and the match provided there is a margin of two points over the opponent(s).

3. Deciding Match Tie-break (10 Points)

When the score in a match is one set all, or two sets all in best of five sets matches, one tie-break game shall be played to decide the match. This tie-break game replaces the deciding final set.

The player/team who first wins ten points shall win this match tie-break and the match provided there is a margin of two points over the opponent(s).

Note: When using the deciding match tie-break to replace the final set:

— the original order of service continues. (Rules 5 and 14)

— in doubles, the order of serving and receiving within the team may be altered, as in the beginning of each set. (Rules 14 and 15)

— before the start of the deciding match tie-break there shall be a 120 seconds set break.

— balls should not be changed before the start of the deciding match tie-break even if a ball change is due.

Appendix V
Role of Court Officials

The referee is the final authority on all questions of tennis law and the referee's decision is final.

In matches where a chair umpire is assigned, the chair umpire is the final authority on all questions of fact during the match. The players have the right to call the referee to court if they disagree with a chair umpire's interpretation of tennis law.

In matches where line umpires and net umpires are assigned, they make all calls (including foot-fault calls) relating to that line or net. The chair umpire has the right to overrule a line umpire or a net umpire if the chair umpire is sure that a clear mistake has been made. The chair umpire is responsible for calling any line (including foot-faults) or net where no line umpire or net umpire is assigned.

A line umpire who cannot make a call shall signal this immediately to the chair umpire who shall make a decision. If the line umpire can not make a call, or if there is no line umpire, and the chair umpire can not make a decision on a question of fact, the point shall be replayed.

In team events where the referee is sitting on-court, the referee is also the final authority on questions of fact. Play may be stopped or suspended at any time the chair umpire decides it is necessary or appropriate.

The referee may also stop or suspend play in the case of darkness, weather or adverse court conditions. When play is suspended for darkness, this should be done at the end of a set, or after an even number of games have been played in the set in progress. After a suspension in play, the score and position of players on-court in the match shall stand when the match resumes.

The chair umpire or referee shall make decisions regarding continuous play and coaching in respect of any Code of Conduct that is approved and in operation.

Case 1: The chair umpire awards the server a first service after an overrule, but the receiver argues that it should be a second service, since the server had already served a fault. Should the referee be called to court to give a decision?

Decision: Yes. The chair umpire makes the first decision about questions of tennis law (issues relating to the application of specific facts). However, if a player appeals the chair umpire's decision, then the referee shall be called to make the final decision.

Case 2: A ball is called out, but a player claims that the ball was good. May the referee be called to court to make a decision?

Decision: No. The chair umpire makes the final decision on questions of fact (issues relating to what actually happened during a specific incident).

Case 3: Is a chair umpire allowed to overrule a line umpire at the end of a point if, in the chair umpire's opinion, a clear mistake was made earlier in the point?

Decision: No. A chair umpire may only overrule a line umpire immediately after the clear mistake has been made.

Case 4: A line umpire calls a ball "Out" and then the player argues that the ball was good. Is the chair umpire allowed to overrule the line umpire? Decision: No. A chair umpire must never overrule as the result of the protest or appeal by a player Case 5: A line umpire calls a ball "Out". The chair umpire was unable to see clearly, but thought the ball was in. May the chair umpire overrule the line umpire?

Decision: No. The chair umpire may only overrule when sure that the line umpire made a clear mistake.

Case 6: Is a line umpire allowed to change the call after the chair umpire has announced the score?

Decision: Yes. If a line umpire realises a mistake, a correction should be made as soon as possible provided it is not as the result of a protest or appeal of a player.

Case 7: If a chair umpire or line umpire calls "out" and then corrects the call to good, what is the correct decision?

Decision: The chair umpire must decide if the original "out" call was a hindrance to either player. If it was a hindrance, the point shall be replayed. If it was not a hindrance, the player who hit the ball wins the point.

Case 8: A ball is blown back over the net and the player correctly reaches over the net to try to play the ball. The opponent(s) hinders the player from doing this. What is the correct decision?

Decision: The chair umpire must decide if the hindrance was deliberate or unintentional and either awards the point to the hindered player or order the point to be replayed.

APPENDIX VI

PROCEDURES FOR REVIEW AND HEADINGS ON THE RULES OF TENNIS

1. Introduction

1.1 These procedures were approved by the Board of Directors of the International Tennis Federation ("Board of Directors") on 17 May 1998.

1.2 The Board of Directors may from time to time supplement, amend, or vary these procedures.

2. Objectives

2.1 The International Tennis Federation is the custodian of the Rules of Tennis and is committed to:

a. Preserving the traditional character and integrity of the game of tennis.

b. Actively preserving the skills traditionally required to play the game.

c. Encouraging improvements, which maintain the challenge of the game.

d. Ensuring fair competition.

2.2 To ensure fair, consistent and expeditious review and hearings in relation to the Rules of Tennis the procedures set out below shall apply.

3. Scope

3.1 These Procedures shall apply to Rulings under:

a. Rule 1-The Court.

b. Rule 3-The Ball.

c. Rule 4-The Racket.

d. Appendix I and II of the Rules of Tennis.

e. Any other Rules of Tennis which the International Tennis Federation may decide.

4. Structure

4.1 Under these procedures Rulings shall be issued by a Ruling Board.

4.2 Such Rulings shall be final save, for an entitlement to appeal to an Appeal Tribunal pursuant to these procedures.

5. Application

5.1 Rulings shall be taken either:

a. Following a motion of the Board of Directors; or

b. Upon the receipt of an application in accordance with the procedures set out below.

6. Appointment and Composition of Ruling Boards

6.1 Ruling Boards shall be appointed by the President of the International Tennis Federation ("President") or his designee and shall comprise of such a number, as the President or his designee shall determine.

6.2 If more than one person is appointed to the Ruling Board the Ruling Board shall nominate one person from amongst themselves to act as Chairperson.

6.3 The Chairperson shall be entitled to regulate the procedures prior to and at any review and/or hearing of a Ruling Board.

7. Proposed Rulings by the Ruling Board

7.1 The details of any proposed Ruling issued upon the motion of the Board of Directors may be provided to any bona fide person or any players, equipment manufacturer or national association or members thereof with an interest in the proposed Ruling.

7.2 Any person so notified shall be given a reasonable period within which to forward comments, objections, or requests for information to the President or his designee in connection with the proposed Ruling.

8. Application for Ruling

8.1 An application for a Ruling may be made by any party with a bona fide interest in the Ruling including any player, equipment manufacturer or national association or member thereof.

8.2 Any application for a Ruling must be submitted in writing to the President.

8.3 To be valid an application for a Ruling must include the following minimum information:

a. The full name and address of the Applicant.

b. The date of the application.

c. A statement clearly identifying the interest of the Applicant in the question upon which a Ruling is requested.

d. All relevant documentary evidence upon which the Applicant intends to rely at any hearing.

e. If, in the opinion of the Applicant, expert evidence is necessary he shall include a request for such expert evidence to be heard. Such request must identify the name of any expert proposed and their relevant expertise.

f. When an application for a Ruling on a racket or other piece of equipment is made, a prototype or, exact, copy of the equipment in question must be submitted with the application for a Ruling.

g. If, in the opinion of the Applicant, there are extraordinary or unusual circumstances, which require a Ruling to be made within a specified time or before a specified date he shall include a statement describing the extraordinary or unusual circumstances.

8.4 If an application for a Ruling does not contain the information and/or equipment referred to at Clause 8.3 (a)-(g) above the President or his designee shall notify the Applicant giving the Applicant a specified reasonable time within which to remedy the defect. If the Applicant fails to remedy the defect within the specified time the application shall be dismissed.

9. Convening the Ruling Board

9.1 On receipt of a valid application or on the motion of the Board of Directors the President or his designee may convene a Ruling Board to deal with the application or motion.

9.2 The Ruling Board need not hold a hearing to deal with an application or motion where the application or motion, in the opinion of the Chairperson can be resolved in a fair manner without a hearing.

10. Procedure of the Ruling Board

10.1 The Chairperson of a Ruling Board shall determine the appropriate form, procedure and date of any review and/or hearing.

10.2 The Chairperson shall provide written notice of those matters set out at 10.1 above to any Applicant or any person or association who has expressed an interest in the proposed Ruling.

10.3 The Chairperson shall determine all matters relating to evidence and shall not be bound by judicial rules governing procedure and admissibility of evidence provided that the review and/or hearing is conducted in a fair manner with a reasonable opportunity for the relevant parties to present their case.

10.4 Under these procedures any review and/or hearings:

a. Shall take place in private.

b. May be adjourned and/or postponed by the Ruling Board.

10.5 The Chairperson shall have the discretion to co-opt from time to time additional members onto the Ruling Board with special skill or experience to deal with specific issues, which require such special skill or experience.

10.6 The Ruling Board shall take its decision by a simple majority. No member of the Ruling Board may abstain.

10.7 The Chairperson shall have the complete discretion to make such order against the Applicant [and/or other individuals or organisations commenting objecting or requesting information at any review and/or hearing] in relation to the costs of the application and/or the reasonable expenses incurred by the Ruling Board in holding tests or obtaining reports relating to equipment subject to a Ruling as he shall deem appropriate.

11. Notification

11.1 Once a Ruling Board has reached a decision it shall provide written notice to the Applicant, or, any person or association who has expressed an interest in the proposed Ruling as soon as reasonably practicable.

11.2 Such written notice shall include a summary of the reasoning behind the decision of the Ruling Board.

11.3 Upon notification to the Applicant or upon such other date specified by the Ruling Board the Ruling of the Ruling Board shall be immediately binding under the Rules of Tennis.

12. Application of Current Rules of Tennis

12.1 Subject to the power of the Ruling Board to issue interim Rulings the current Rules of Tennis shall continue to apply until any review and/or hearing of the Ruling Board is concluded and a Ruling issued by the Ruling Board.

12.2 Prior to and during any review and/or hearing the Chairperson of the Ruling Board may issue such directions as are deemed reasonably necessary in the implementation of the Rules of Tennis and of these procedures including the issue of interim Rulings.

12.3 Such interim Rulings may include restraining orders on the use of any equipment under the Rules of Tennis pending a Ruling by the Ruling Board as to whether or not the equipment meets the specification of the Rules of Tennis.

13. Appointment and Composition of Appeal Tribunals

13.1 Appeal Tribunals shall be appointed by the President or his designee from [members of the Board of Directors/Technical Commission].

13.2 No member of the Ruling Board who made the original Ruling shall be a member of the Appeal Tribunal.

13.3 The Appeal Tribunal shall comprise of such number as the President or his designee shall determine but shall be no less than three.

13.4 The Appeal Tribunal shall nominate one person from amongst themselves to act as Chairperson.

13.5 The Chairperson shall be entitled to regulate the procedures prior to and at any appeal hearing.

14. Application to Appeal

14.1 An Applicant [or a person or association who has expressed an interest and forwarded any comments, objections, or requests to a proposed Ruling] may appeal any Ruling of the Ruling Board.

14.2 To be valid an application for an appeal must be:

a. Made in writing to the Chairperson of the Ruling Board who made the Ruling appealed not later than [45] days following notification of the Ruling;

b. Must set out details of the Ruling appealed against; and

c. Must contain the full grounds of the appeal.

14.3 Upon receipt of a valid application to appeal the Chairperson of the Ruling Board making the original Ruling may require a reasonable appeal fee to be paid by the Appellant as a condition of appeal. Such appeal fee shall be repaid to the Appellant if the appeal is successful.

15. Convening the Appeal Tribunal

15.1 The President or his designee shall convene the Appeal Tribunal following payment by the Appellant of any appeal fee.

16. Procedures of Appeal Tribunal

16.1 The Appeal Tribunal and their Chairperson shall conduct procedures and hearings in accordance with those matters set out in sections 10, 11 and 12 above.

16.2 Upon notification to the Appellant or upon such other date specified by the Appeal Tribunal the Ruling of the Appeal Tribunal shall be immediately binding and final under the Rules of Tennis.

17. General

17.1 If a Ruling Board consists of only one member that single member shall be responsible for regulating the hearing as Chairperson and shall determine the procedures to be followed prior to and during any review and/or hearing.

17.2 All review and/or hearings shall be conducted in English. In any hearing where an Applicant, and/or other individuals or organisations commenting, objecting or requesting information do not speak English an interpreter must be present. Wherever practicable the interpreter shall be independent.

17.3 The Ruling Board or Appeal Tribunal may publish extracts from its own Rulings.

17.4 All notifications to be made pursuant to these procedures shall be in writing.

17.5 Any notifications made pursuant to these procedures shall be deemed notified upon the date that they were communicated, sent or transmitted to the Applicant or other relevant party.

17.6 A Ruling Board shall have the discretion to dismiss an application if in its reasonable opinion the application is substantially similar to an application or motion upon which a Ruling Board has made a decision and/or Ruling within the 36 months prior to the date of the application. The following procedure is for the usual combined doubles and singles court. (See note at foot for a court for one purpose only). First select the position of the net; a

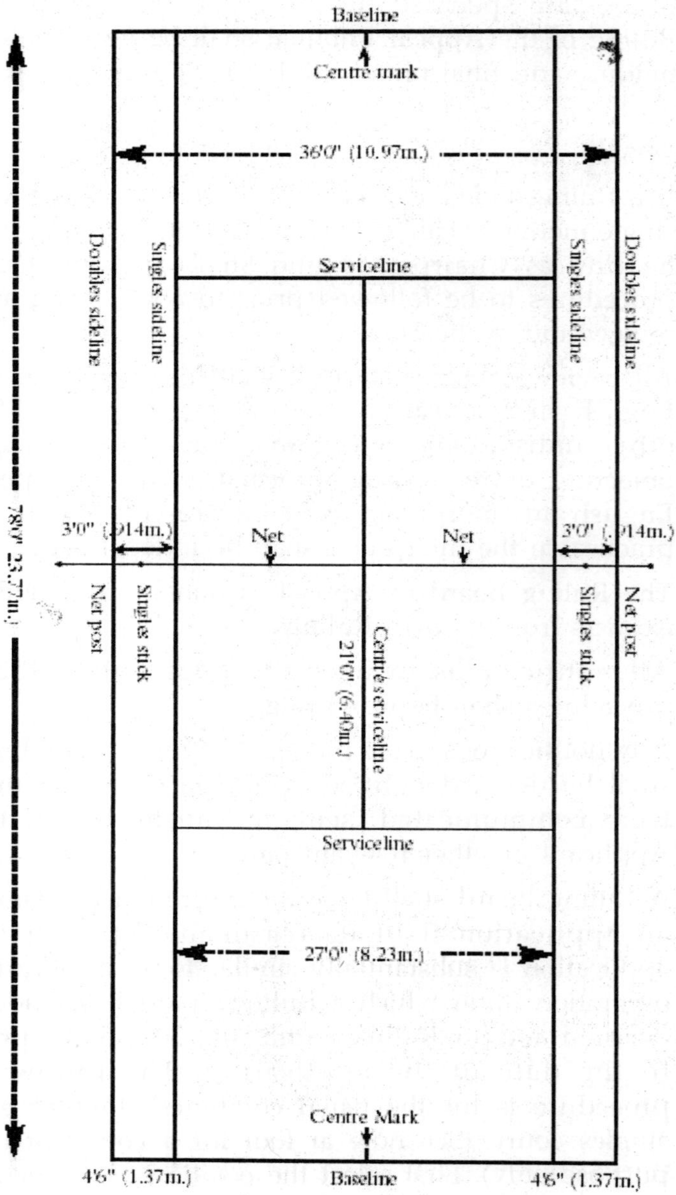
Baseline
Centre mark
36'0" (10.97m.)
Doubles sideline
Singles sideline
Serviceline
Singles sideline
Doubles sideline
78'0" 23.77m.)
3'0" (.914m.)
Net
Net
3'0" (.914m.)
Net post
Singles stick
Centre serviceline
21'0" (6.40m.)
Singles stick
Net post
Serviceline
27'0" (8.23m.)
Centre Mark
4'6" (1.37m.)
Baseline
4'6" (1.37m.)

Figure 1

straight line 42 feet (12.8 m) long. Mark the centre (X on the diagram above) and, measuring from there in each direction, mark: at 13'6" (4.11 m) the points a, b, where the net crosses the inner sidelines, at 16'6" (5.03 m) the positions of the singles sticks (n, n), at 18'0" (5.48 m) the points A, B, where the net crosses the outer sidelines, at 21'0" (6.40 m) the positions of the net posts (N, N), being the ends of the original 42'0" (12.8 m) line.

Insert pegs at A and B and attach to them the respective ends of two measuring tapes. On one, which will measure the diagonal of the half-court,take a length 53'1" (16.18 m) and on the other (to measure the sideline) a length of 39'0" (11.885 m). Pull both taut so that at these distances they meet at a point C, which is one corner of the court. Reverse the measurements to find the other corner D. As a check on this operation it is advisable at this stage to verify the length of the line CD which, being the baseline, should be found to be 36'0" (10.97m); and at the same time its centre J can be marked, and also the ends of the inner sidelines (c, d), 4'6" (1.37 m) from C and D. The centreline and serviceline are now marked by means of the points F, H, G, which are measured 21'0" (6.40 m) from the net down the lines bc, XJ, ad, respectively.

Identical procedure the other side of the net completes the court. If a singles court only is required, no lines are necessary outside the points a, b, c, d, but the court can be measured out as above. Alternatively, the corners of the baseline (c, d) can be found if preferred by pegging the two tapes at a and b instead of at A and B, and by then using lengths of 47'5" (14.46 m) and 39'0" (11.885 m). The net posts will be at n, n, and a 33'0" (10 m) singles net should be used.

When a combined doubles and singles court with a doubles net is used for singles, the net must be supported at the points n, n, to a height of 3 feet 6 inches (1.07 m) by means of two singles sticks, which shall be not more than 3 inches (7.5 cm) square or 3 inches (7.5 cm) in diameter. The centres of the singles sticks shall be 3 feet (.914 m) outside the singles court on each side.

To assist in the placing of these singles sticks it is desirable that the points n, n, should each be shown with a white dot when the court is marked. Note: As a guide for international competitions, the recommended minimum distance between the baselines and the backstops should be 21 feet (6.40 m) and between the sidelines and the sidestops the recommended minimum distance should be 12 feet (3.66 m).

As a guide for recreational and Club play, the recommended minimum distance between the baselines and the backstops should be 18 feet (5.48 m) and between the sidelines and the sidestops the recommended minimum distance should be 10 feet (3.05 m).

As a guide, the recommended minimum height to the ceiling should be 30 feet (9.14 m).

Suggestions on How to Mark out a Court

The following procedure is for the usual combined doubles and singles court. (See note at foot for a court for one purpose only). First select the position of the net; a straight line 42 feet (12.8 m) long. Mark the centre (X on the diagram above) and, measuring from there in each direction, mark: at 13'6" (4.11 m) the points a, b, where the net crosses the inner sidelines, at 16'6" (5.03 m) the positions of the singles sticks (n, n), at 18'0" (5.48 m) the points A, B, where the net crosses the outer sidelines, at 21'0" (6.40 m) the positions of the net posts (N, N), being the ends of the original 42'0" (12.8 m) line.

Insert pegs at A and B and attach to them the respective ends of two measuring tapes. On one, which will measure the diagonal of the half-court,take a length 53'1" (16.18 m) and on the other (to measure the sideline) a length of 39'0" (11.885 m). Pull both taut so that at these distances they meet at a point C, which is one corner of the court. Reverse the measurements to find the other corner D. As a check on this operation it is advisable at this stage to verify the length of the line CD which, being the baseline, should be found to be 36'0" (10.97m); and at the same time its centre J can be marked, and also the ends of the inner sidelines (c, d), 4'6" (1.37 m) from C and D. The centreline and serviceline are now marked by means of the points F, H, G, which are measured 21'0" (6.40 m) from the net down the lines bc, XJ, ad, respectively.

Identical procedure the other side of the net completes the court. If a singles court only is required, no lines are necessary outside the points a, b, c, d, but the court can be measured out as above. Alternatively, the corners of the baseline (c, d) can be found if preferred by pegging the two tapes at a and b instead of at A and B, and by then using lengths of 47'5" (14.46 m) and 39'0" (11.885 m). The net posts will be at n, n, and a 33'0" (10 m) singles net should be used.

When a combined doubles and singles court with a doubles net is used for singles, the net must be supported at the points n, n, to a height of 3 feet 6 inches (1.07 m) by means of two singles sticks, which shall be not more than 3 inches (7.5 cm) square or 3 inches (7.5 cm) in diameter. The centres of the singles sticks shall be 3 feet (.914 m) outside the singles court on each side.

To assist in the placing of these singles sticks it is desirable that the points n, n, should each be shown with a white dot when the court is marked. Note: As a guide for international competitions, the recommended minimum distance between the baselines and the backstops should be 21 feet (6.40 m) and between the sidelines and the sidestops the recommended minimum distance should be 12 feet (3.66 m).

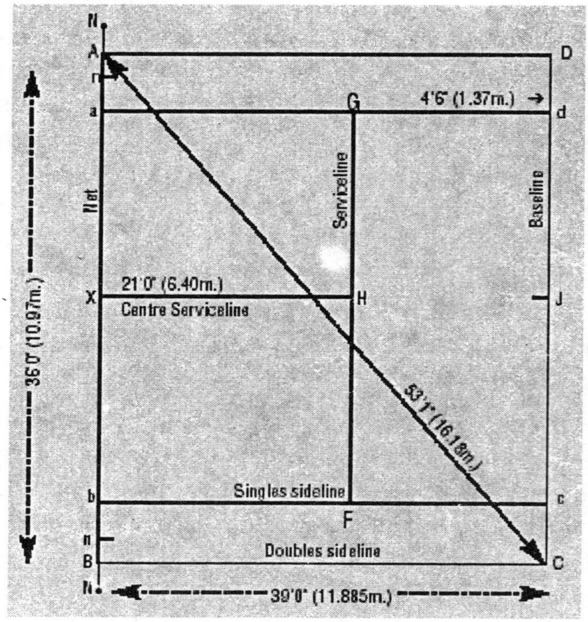

Figure 2.

As a guide for recreational and Club play, the recommended minimum distance between the baselines and the backstops should be 18 feet (5.48 m) and between the sidelines and the sidestops the recommended minimum distance should be 10 feet (3.05 m).

As a guide, the recommended minimum height to the ceiling should be 30 feet (9.14 m).

Bibliography

Alfred Watson, *Young Sportsman,* Lawrence & Bullen; 1st Edition; 663 pages, 1900

Braden V. and B. Bruns, *Vic Braden's Tennis for the Future,* 1977.

Brian Glanville, Puffin, *Puffin Book of Tennis,* 1st Paperback Edition; 156 pages, 1981

Bud Collins' *Modern Encyclopedia of Tennis*—Edited By Bud Collins & Zander Hollander. Doubleday; 1980

_______________, *Total Tennis: The Ultimate Tennis Encyclopedia,* Sport Media Publishing, Bud Collins, 1980

Chris Bowers, *Book of Tennis,* JWM Publishing; Softcover Edition; 192 pages, 2003

Darren Christison, *Tennis Companion 1990/91,* GMG Sport; Australian Softcover Edition; 60 pages, 1990

David Emery, *Who's Who In International Tennis,* Sphere Books, 1983

Frank Phelps & Gordy Sabine, *Tennis Bibliography 1874-2000,* 1st US Edition; 377 pages, 2004

Gallwey, W. T., *The Inner Game of Tennis,* 1974.

Gerald Gurney. *Tennis Squash And Badminton Bygones,* Shire; 1st Paperback Edition; 32 pages, 1984

Haylett, J& R Evans, *Illustrated Encyclopaedia of World Tennis,* Waymark; 1989

ITF, *Men's Results Guide Wimbledon 1995*, Softcover Edition; 340 pages, June 1995

_______________, *Men's Results Guide Wimbledon 1996*, Softcover Edition; 348 pages, June 1996

_______________, *Men's Results Guide Wimbledon 1997*, Softcover Edition, June 1997

_______________, *Men's Results Guide Wimbledon 1998*, Softcover Edition, June 1998

______________, *Men's Results Guide Wimbledon 2003,* Softcover Edition; 238 pages, June 2003

______________, *Men's Results Guide Wimbledon 2005,* Softcover Edition; 227 pages, June 2005

______________, *Women's Results Guide Wimbledon 2005,* Softcover Edition; 203 pages, June 2005

Jeanne Cherry, *Tennis Antiques And Collectibles,* Amaryllis Press; 1995

John Parsons, *Ultimate Encyclopedia Of Tennis: The Definitive Illustrated Guide To World Tennis,* Hodder & Stoughton; 1st Edition; 224 pages, 1998

Lance Tingay, *Guinness Book of Tennis Facts and Feats,* Guinness Superlatives; 1983.

Larry Lorimer, *Tennis Book,* Random House; 1st US Softcover Edition; 160 pages, 1980

Martin Hedges, *Concise Dictionary of Tennis,* Bison; 1st Edition; 278 pages, 1978

Maurice Brady, *Encyclopaedia of Lawn Tennis,* Robert Hale; 1st Edition; 179 pages, 1958

______________, *Lawn Tennis Encyclopaedia,* David & Charles; 1969

Max Robertson, *Encyclopedia of Tennis*—Edited by George Allen & Unwin; 1st Edition; 392 pages, 1974

Norman Giller Edited by *Book Of Tennis,* LISTS- Sidgwick & Jackson; 1985

Ossian Shine, *Language of Tennis,* Carcanet Press; 2003

Peter Schwed, *How To Talk Tennis,* Galahad Books; US Edition; 143 pages, 1996

Reginald Brace, David & Charles, *Sportsviewers Guide: Tennis,* 1st Edition; 64 pages, 1984

Robert Everitt, Racket Sports Collectibles - Schiffer Books; 2003 1st US Edition; 307 pages.

Schikel R., *The World of Tennis,* 1975.

Siegfried Kuebler, *Book of Tennis Rackets from the Beginning of the 16th Century to about 1990,* Kuebler; 2000

Staff of Uslta, *United States Lawn Tennis Association Official Encyclopedia Of Tennis,* Edited By Harper & Row; 1972 1st US Edition; 472 pages.

